Hilde

With best wishes

and many thanks for
all your help in the
past

[signature]

September 1976.

Penguin Education

Case Studies in Decision Analysis
P. G. Moore, H. Thomas, D. W. Bunn, and Juliet Hampton

Modern Management Texts

General Editor:

D. S. Pugh

Operational Sciences Editor:

P. G. Moore

P. G. Moore, H. Thomas, D. W. Bunn,
and Juliet Hampton

Case Studies in
Decision Analysis

Penguin Education

Penguin Books Ltd,
Harmondsworth, Middlesex, England
Penguin Books,
625 Madison Avenue, New York, New York 10022, U.S.A.
Penguin Books Australia Ltd,
Ringwood, Victoria, Australia
Penguin Books Canada Ltd,
41 Steelcase Road West, Markham, Ontario, Canada
Penguin Books (N.Z.) Ltd,
182–190 Wairau Road, Auckland 10, New Zealand

First published 1976
Copyright © P. G. Moore, H. Thomas, D. W. Bunn, and
Juliet Hampton, 1976

Made and printed in Great Britain by
Hazell Watson & Viney Ltd,
Aylesbury, Bucks
Set in Monotype Times

Contents

Preface

This volume has a number of distinctive features, and a few words of explanation are needed as to its origins, purpose, and possible methods of use. Two of us (PGM and HT) have been working in the field of Decision Analysis for some years. Decision analysis can be briefly defined as being a systematic approach to decision-making in situations where there are a number of alternative courses of action and some uncertainty as to the precise outcomes of the various possible options. In the course of our work in this field, we have deliberately involved ourselves in the extensive study of practical problem situations and have, in consequence, obtained a great deal of experience of applications in a wide variety of fields. This includes such areas as the public and private sectors, service and manufacturing industries, large and small organizations.

In 1971 the Social Sciences Research Council gave us a grant to extend our work on the applied side of decision analysis, and as a major priority we have drawn up, with the aid of DWB and JH, a series of case studies or case histories based on our experiences. These bring out many of the issues and problems which can be tackled through the application of the tools of decision analysis. The present volume provides a selection from these studies. The aim has been twofold. Firstly, we believe there is sufficient practical realism in the examples presented to enable the practitioner, or would-be practitioner, to explore and test the methods of decision analysis. To guide the reader, the opening item is a concise account of the principles of decision analysis illustrated by a worked example. Secondly, it is hoped that these studies will assist the practising manager in defining the wide range of situations where the basic principles of decision analysis can be fruitfully applied. Each case in the text has sufficient background to demonstrate the real nature of the problem situation. Enough guidance is given to indicate the manner in which the problem can be structured and the methods available for tackling the analysis.

We believe that several important benefits flow from studying these cases. Firstly, they raise the real issues concerned in problem situations. Secondly, they show the relevance of the concepts of decision analysis to a full understanding of decision problems. Thirdly, they encourage consideration in some depth of the question of implementation, a feature which is lacking in many Management Sciences texts. The particular areas of application given are indicative of the range possible, and other case studies have been, and are being, developed. Thus the current volume provides a good overview of the power and usefulness of the approach in a wide range of situations.

In some of the studies described, the problem is posed and the reader is left to carry through the complete analysis for himself. In other studies, some part or parts of the technical structuring and analysis are carried out in the text and, having mastered the various analyses given, the reader must determine the fundamental issues concerned, perhaps judging how he would use such analyses to assist him in coming to a final decision. A few cases pose some more general issues that the reader will wish to consider as being applicable to a wide class of decisions. The volume includes not only discussions of decision analyses pursued but also detailed reviews of the assessment and use of subjective probabilities and utilities, the use of simulation techniques, multi-attribute objectives, bidding models, etc. Nobody reading this volume could seriously dispute our view that decision analysis provides a framework for tackling a fascinating range of important and complex business problems.

There are not, of course, precise answers to most of the cases discussed in this volume as there would be for routine algebraic problems. Hence we have decided against the idea of providing any formal solutions as this would detract from the educational value of the volume as we perceive it. In the introduction, however, we have given a few notes on each of the ten cases that have been included. These notes serve two distinct purposes. In the first place, they enable the reader to see at a quick glance the nature of the problem under discussion and the particular background from which the case is drawn. Secondly, they give some guidance as to the way or ways in which the analysis or appreciation of the case might fruitfully proceed, and highlight some of the general issues raised. A companion volume on the principles of decision analysis (by P. G. Moore and H. Thomas), entitled *The Anatomy of Decisions*, is being published by Penguin in the same series.

Finally, it is appropriate that we should thank all those organizations and individuals with whom we have worked for their help in the course of preparation of this volume. In particular we would thank Mr G. Easton and Mr R. C. Bell for their assistance on the Quantock and Harman Merchants cases, Messrs L. D. Phillips, J. A. Morris and the Glacier Metal Company for help with the Hewitt Ingott case, and Messrs R. E. Cox and M. Whitney for their help with the Automatic Landing System case.

All the cases are based on real-life situations with which we have been personally involved, although some changes have occasionally been made, either for security reasons or to make the case more manageable within the compass of a volume like this. We are grateful to students at the London Business School who have acted as guinea pigs for drafts of the various cases, and to the organizations concerned for permission to publish the material obtained from our collaboration with them.

P. G. MOORE
H. THOMAS
D. W. BUNN
JULIET HAMPTON
London Graduate School of Business Studies, 1974

Introduction

This introduction provides some notes on each of the eleven items included in this volume, drawing attention to the basic nature of each item, indicating how the analysis might fruitfully proceed and suggesting extra references to methodology that might be of value.

(1) How to make a choice

This is a descriptive piece that seeks to outline the basic principles of decision analysis. It introduces the ideas of expected monetary value (EMV), the expected value of perfect information (EVPI), and the procedure whereby probabilities are revised in the light of extra information. The ideas are discussed and illustrated around a problem of launching a possible new product.

Further reading on the principles of decision analysis is contained in the references listed at the end of this introduction.

(2) Harman Merchants

This case describes, in some detail, a reorganization situation facing a builders' merchants that had to be resolved within a period of some four months. After describing the background to the situation, a broad consideration of alternatives is made, leading to seven strategies being considered in depth. Some discussion ensues on the uncertainties and how they should be estimated, followed by a detailed consideration of the calculation of the appropriate Net Present Values (NPVs). The reader is left to construct appropriate decision trees and to analyse them by the standard 'roll-back' procedure.

(3) The Introduction of an Automatic Landing System

This case describes a situation faced by the National Air Traffic Services in 1968. It provides an example of a situation that is quasi-governmental in nature, involving information inputs from a number of different sources. The reader has first to extract and structure the various alternatives, basically three in number, facing NATS. Secondly, the various probabilities and values need to be decided and, finally, the constructed decision tree has to be analysed on the roll-back procedure to obtain the best initial decision. Readers are also asked to consider the sensitivity of the decision to the initial assessments of the correctness of the advice received in 1968.

(4) Aeropa Ltd

This company, engaged on research, development, and production of both civil and military aircraft, is in financial difficulties. In particular a large loan has to be repaid shortly. The Board is exploring various options open to them for handling this situation, and two in particular are being discussed in some detail. Readers are required to extract from the dialogue of the five managers concerned the necessary inputs in order to examine the alternatives facing Aeropa, using a decision analysis approach. This requires turning some of the subjective opinions into more formal assessments for the purpose of analysis.

(5) Quantock Plastics

This case concerns a company manufacturing plastic film that is offered the chance of buying, at a favourable price, a second-hand co-extrusion casting machine. The decision hinges critically on the uncertainties regarding market demands for the film, and a decision is required within the space of two to three weeks. A great deal of information is compiled by the project team concerned with the problem, and the reader is left with the need to sort out the data and extract from it a meaningful solution on decision analysis lines. The basic lessons to be learnt from the case are the structuring of the problem and the use of EMV as the criterion of choice.

(6) Maybury Company

The Maybury Company is considering the decision as to whether or not to launch a new product line. In addition to their own information the possible value of 'buying in' the services of an external market-research bureau is being considered. The case discusses two approaches to the problem. The first approach approximates the new product's likely performance in terms of discrete figures and goes on to evaluate a bound on the value of additional information. The second approach introduces the concept of continuous distributions to describe the prevailing opinion concerning the product's likely share of the market, and incorporates this into an analysis to describe the likely effect of the additional information on that opinion.

The case requires readers to analyse a fairly complex situation involving the revision of probabilities. It discusses the ability of a discrete distribution to approximate effectively a continuous distribution, and raises a number of issues in connection with probability assessments in a practical situation.

(7) Hewitt Ingot Co.

This case study illustrates how decision analysis can be applied to the type of decision problem in which similar decisions have to be made over a period of time. At monthly intervals, executives within Hewitt Ingot have to decide to 'stock' or 'sell' that part of the productive output known as 'recovered melts'. Recovered melts can be used profitably within the company in the production of particular types of ingots, provided that the stockholding costs are not excessive. In other words, it is crucial that the melts in stock should be sufficient to meet immediate or very short-term demands from within the company but not so large as to incur a medium- to long-term investment loss to the company. In the latter case immediate disposal of the melts would be more beneficial to the company. Many models have been suggested to handle this kind of dynamic programming problem. Its structure is similar to decision problems that arise in research and development management where research executives have to select particular R & D projects at regular time intervals for inclusion within R & D portfolios. Equally in the area of financial planning such a formulation can be applied to repetitive investment decisions.

(8) Property Redevelopment in Caracas

This case is based upon an investment problem facing a large banking organization in 1970. The bank was about to move to a new head office and had to decide how best to re-utilize its present office block. Should it be sold outright or redeveloped into shops, apartments, offices, or a hotel? Some of these options offered high expectations of future revenues but with correspondingly higher risks. An important aspect of the analysis is therefore the measurement of the organization's attitude towards risk.

For the analytical treatment of risk within an investment situation the reader is referred to Wagle (1967). Raiffa (1968) discusses the general basis of risk and utility in decision theory, whilst the use of drawing from an urn with a defined proportion of red and black balls to estimate probabilities is also described in Exhibit 4 of the Harman Merchants case. The capital investment procedures used in this case are discussed in more detail in Merrett and Sykes (1966).

(9) Aztech Electronics

This case is centred around the evaluation which Aztech Electronics had to make in 1968 of a set of ten research and development projects which had come up for review. The issues arising, however, necessarily range much more widely to cover the whole process by which research and development projects are selected in Aztech. For example, it is crucial to decide upon the criterion with which to evaluate a project. From a purely financial point of view, should Net Present Value, Internal Rate of Return, or Payback be adopted? In order to incorporate elements of uncertainty into these financial criteria, the risk simulation approach advocated by Hertz (1964) was utilized.

It is clear that research and development investments should not be evaluated just on financial criteria, but other factors should be considered as well. A multi-dimensional approach is used to evaluate the projects. Apart from reconciling the project scores on different criteria, the overall research and development process in Aztech leads to a consensus problem in reconciling evaluations from several individuals. Raiffa (1968) discusses aspects of this problem.

(10) J. Sainsbury Ltd

The Sainsbury and Whernside cases are each concerned with competitive bidding, and have therefore been grouped together. However, the nature of the bidding problem is significantly different in each. Sainsburys, a major supermarket chain in Great Britain, found themselves in a competitive bidding situation a few years ago, when they were invited to tender for a haul of butter which had been impounded at the Port of London. Although such a unique situation allowed Sainsburys to take a purely marginal approach to the problem, they were faced with a great deal of uncertainty, precisely because it was such an unusual situation. The case carries through a great deal of the analysis, but leaves the reader to decide upon the precise bid that he would recommend Sainsburys to make.

(11) Whernside Construction Ltd

Whernside presents a rather different form of bidding case. It is a major British construction company for which competitive bidding is a way of life. This underlying problem is one of developing a bidding strategy that will maximize long-term objectives. The case discusses a number of aspects of repetitive competitive bidding and raises a number of issues for the reader to consider, concerning cost estimates, utility functions, and competitive behaviour.

References

HERTZ, D. B., 'Risk Analysis in Capital Investment', *Harvard Business Review*, 1964.

LINDLEY, D. V., *Making Decisions*, Wiley, 1971.

MERRETT, A. J., and SYKES, A., *Capital Budgeting and Company Finance*, Longmans, 1966.

MOORE, P. G., *Risk in Business Decision*, Longmans, 1972.

RAIFFA, H., *Decision Theory: Introductory Lectures on Choices under Uncertainty*, Addison-Wesley, 1968.

THOMAS, H., *Decision Theory and the Manager*, Pitman, 1972.

WAGLE, B. V., 'A Statistical Analysis of Risk in Capital Investment Projects', *Operational Research Quarterly*, Vol. 18, No. 1, 1967.

1 How to Make a Choice

Introduction

In the past twenty years, a number of new techniques have been developed for the use of business managers, while many existing techniques have been broadened almost beyond recognition through the extensive development of electronic computing. Although many, if not most, of these techniques are essentially simple in concept, they have often been sponsored by over-enthusiastic specialists, and managers have consequently sometimes regarded them with a certain degree of suspicion and discomfort. Part of this reaction is related to the attitude of mind which regards judgement and intuition as the primary elements in solving a business or administrative problem, as opposed to a problem in, say, physical research. The intense and sustained effort required for progress in subjects like physics, it is argued, would not be worthwhile in business, because the relevant data in the business problem would never be known with sufficient accuracy or certainty to justify hard thought.

Two pertinent factors have been overlooked. Firstly, the inaccuracies or uncertainties in the data could perhaps themselves be precisely specified, so that their very existence would provide an incentive for hard thinking. Uncertainty exists in virtually all problem situations. We need to be able to cope with it, to eliminate it where possible, but to live with it in the most efficient manner when it cannot be eliminated. Many executives think of themselves as individuals whose greater grasp of the available information and greater insights remove the uncertainty from the situation. Even casual observation of most business decisions usually reveals the fallacy of this view; substantial uncertainty is more often the rule than the exception.

Secondly, hard thought should enable the manager to reduce a large messy problem with many variables and factors to one where the issues, although not soluble by the use of techniques alone, are focused on fewer variables and factors. The area within which judgement is required is then more sharply defined. Of course, this means that judgement on specific issues becomes more important and more observable. But such an approach ensures that a top manager's task is not cluttered with matters that can be resolved in other ways. This reserves his energy, time and expertise for issues which cannot readily be delegated. The need for consistent and coherent decision-making is paramount in most organizations. There is, if these lines of argument are pursued, a greater number of problem situations than commonly admitted where basic scientific methods, as in decision analysis, can be effectively employed with the promise of substantial reward.

In putting forward any form of logical approach, the structure for solving the problem must first be decided. Firstly, what is the *objective*? Secondly, what are the *alternative* actions which are open? Thirdly, what are the possible *outcomes* of each action and their *likelihoods*? Finally, the nature and form of the objective will provide a yardstick by which the outcomes of the particular decision problem can be measured; and the *criteria* to be used in choosing between alternatives must be selected.

Expected Monetary Value

Decision theory uses as its basic criterion for choice the concept of expectation. Suppose an airport car park (for cars parked up to twenty-four hours) has the following tariff:

up to two hours	20p
two to four hours	40p
four to twelve hours	80p
over twelve hours	£1·00

Furthermore, the estimated proportional demands for the four categories of parking are 0·4, 0·2, 0·2 and 0·2 respectively. The expected income per car parked is calculated by weighting each element of the tariff by the proportional demand factors. In the present instance, this gives:

expected fee per car parked (in pence) =
$0.4 \times 20 + 0.2 \times 40 + 0.2 \times 80 + 0.2 \times 100 = 52$

The basis of decision theory is that, in comparing this tariff with some alternative (possibly with different estimated demands as well as parking fees), the choice between the alternatives would be based on selecting the tariff with the greater expectation. This is sometimes referred to as the EMV approach, where EMV stands for *expected monetary value*. Note that this is a method of choice; it is not saying that the expectation will always be precisely attained. Indeed, in many instances it cannot be, and this would be true in the above example, since the fee for a single car cannot be precisely 52p. But in the long run average income per car parked should approximate 52p.

The Product Launch

In a simplified form, here is a problem relating to the possible launch of a new product. Simplifications have been made to reduce the discussion to an acceptable length, but they do not affect the general principles concerned. A firm has developed a new product and, after some preliminary consumer studies, the marketing director reviews the situation by making some estimates of profit and loss resulting from the achievement of differing market share levels of 10 per cent or 2 per cent respectively. The costs involved in dropping the product are put at zero, on the argument that development costs for the new product are sunk and are not relevant to current decision-making. Table 1.1 also gives the marketing manager's prior estimates of the chances of achieving the various levels of market share, at the price proposed. (Although the problem has only two levels of market share involved, the methodology would remain the same if, more realistically, a greater number of levels of market share were considered.) Note, too, that the sum of the likelihoods add to unity – thus indicating that these cover the total possible range of outcomes to be considered.

Table 1.1 Payoffs for Initial Decision (£000)

| Decisions | 10% (market share levels) 2% | |
	(0·7 chance)	(0·3 chance)
Launch product	100	−50
Drop product	0	0

Immediate analysis on the lines of the parking case gives:

EMV (Launch) $= 100 \times 0 \cdot 7 - 50 \times 0 \cdot 3 = 55$

whilst

EMV (Drop) $= 0$

Hence, on the basis of selecting the action with the higher EMV, the decision would be to launch the product. Notice, however, that there is still a 30-per-cent chance that launch will, with hindsight, turn out to have been the wrong decision. An important question to ask after such an analysis, commonly referred to as a prior analysis, is whether it is worthwhile to collect some additional market research information that will throw further light upon the probability assessments for market share before taking the final decision. The way to determine the benefits of such research is to compare the expected monetary value of what appears to be the optimum decision after research, less the cost of the research, with the expected monetary value of the apparently best act before research. If the first expected net gain after research is greater than the latter (and positive), then the market research information is economically worthwhile.

Perfect Information

To help set limits on the value of the research, it is useful to consider first of all what would happen with 'perfect information'. The expected profit under conditions of certainty is that which would be realized if the best decision is taken for each market share that actually materializes. Thus, if a market share of 10 per cent is forecast, the optimum decision would be to introduce the new product; if a 2-per-cent market share is forecast, the optimum decision would be to drop the product. So, if you always made the best decision on perfect information, you would launch 70 per cent of the time; the expected monetary value of the optimum decision under these conditions of perfect certainty would therefore be $0 \cdot 7 \times 100 + 0 \cdot 3 \times 0 = 70$.

The difference of 70–55 equivalent to £15,000, between the expected value of the optimum decision under conditions of perfect certainty and that of the optimum decision before any research (based on the subjective probabilities) is called the *expected value of perfect information* or EVPI. This sets the maximum limit on the value obtainable through market research and immediately rules out the spending of more than £15,000, even for a research project which would predict the subsequent market share perfectly. Suppose now that a specific market research proposal for £2,000 is offered to the marketing manager. The proposal offers the option of either test marketing the product or collecting information from consumer panels. After some discussion, the test marketing option seems more favourable, because it can be done extremely quickly. The manager sets out to evaluate the worth of this particular proposal. His basic rule is that the gain in expected monetary value of the optimum decision after the research, over that prevailing before the research, must at least be equal to the cost of that research.

Decision Trees

Before evaluating the problem just posed, it is revealing to structure the problem in a different way. Managers are often interested in a possible sequence of decisions (or problems) which follow one another in some natural order. Such a structure can usefully be presented in a decision tree as in Figure 1.1. The basic concept is that, starting on the left at the point marked 'start' with the set of initial decisions, the possible outcomes and further sets of possible decisions follow each other alternately down each branch of the tree. The next step is to put at the end of each branch of the tree the payoffs, with the test cost inserted on the appropriate branch. This is done in Figure 1.2, where the bottom portion incorporates the earlier analysis, showing at point J an EMV of 55 for launching without test.

Next, market research: the research company says that the market test it is going to carry out will either indicate a high market share (high test) or a low market share (low test). This indication will not, however, be completely reliable in its linkage to 10-per-cent and 2-per-cent market shares, as in the table below, which should be read horizontally.

Now the marketing manager must try to combine the test market results with the original prior estimates of the likelihoods

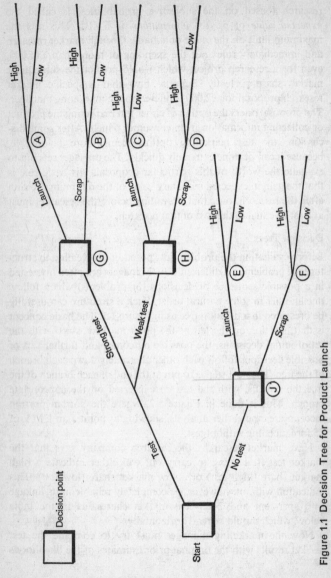

Figure 1.1 Decision Tree for Product Launch

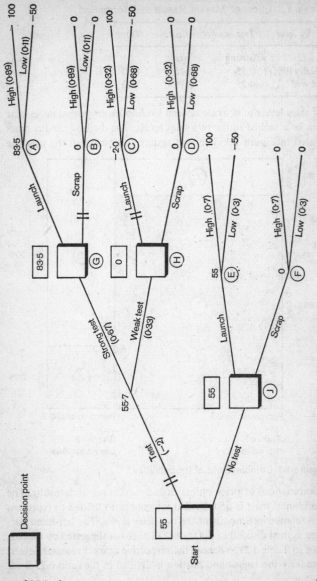

Figure 1.2 Analysis of Decision Tree

Table 1.2 Effect of Market Research Information

Sales level	Test market indication		Totals
	Strong	Weak	
High (10%)	0·85	0·15	1·00
Low (2%)	0·25	0·75	1·00

of sales levels to provide revised likelihoods or probabilities that can be attached to the two sales levels. The method used is illustrated in Figure 1.3. The unit square represents all the possible

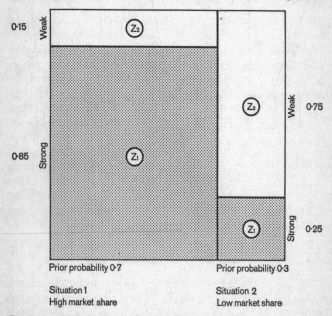

Figure 1.3 Combinations of Probabilities

combinations of prior estimates and market research results. The horizontal scale is first divided into the ratio 0·7:0·3 to represent the relative likelihoods of the two sales levels. The left-hand portion is then divided in the ratio 0·85:0·15 (as suggested by the first row in Table 1.2) to denote the respective market research levels; similarly the right-hand portion is divided in the ratio 0·25:0·75.

The required revised probabilities can be calculated. If the test market gives a strong result, then we must be in the shaded areas of Figure 1.3. By simple areas the proportion relating to the 10-per-cent level (situation I) is:

$$\frac{0 \cdot 7 \times 0 \cdot 85}{0 \cdot 7 \times 0 \cdot 85 + 0 \cdot 25 \times 0 \cdot 3} = 0 \cdot 89$$

that relating to the 2-per-cent level (situation II) will be:

$$\frac{0 \cdot 25 \times 0 \cdot 3}{0 \cdot 7 \times 0 \cdot 85 + 0 \cdot 25 \times 0 \cdot 3} = 0 \cdot 11$$

For weak research results, a similar calculation is done on the unshaded area. This shows that the revised likelihoods corresponding to the 10-per-cent and 2-per-cent levels are $0 \cdot 32$ and $0 \cdot 68$. These have been entered against the appropriate branches of the decision tree in Figure 1.2. With the revised probability assessments, the decision tree can now be formally analysed. The analysis is done on a roll-back principle from right to left. Then at point A in Figure 1.2 the E M V is $0 \cdot 89 \times 100 + 0 \cdot 11 \times (-50)$ $= 83 \cdot 5$ and similarly at point B it is 0. Since the former E M V is the greater, launch is the better decision and the value at G is $83 \cdot 5$, the other route being indicated on the diagram with a double bar. At point C the value is similarly $0 \cdot 32 \times 100 + 0 \cdot 68 \times (-50) = -2$ while at D it is 0. Thus scrap is now the better decision and the value at H is -2. The probability of a strong test indication is $0 \cdot 67$ and that of a weak indication is $0 \cdot 33$. This gives the overall value of the branch as:

$$0 \cdot 67 \times 83 \cdot 5 + 0 \cdot 33 \times 0 - 2 = 53 \cdot 7$$

The expected value of 'not testing' is thus higher, and it is the better decision. Of course this result does not imply that no test market survey is worthwhile. If a survey was a better predictor of the situation, it might be worth doing, depending on the precise relationship between the accuracy expected from the market research and the cost involved.

Interpretation

One final word of caution is appropriate. The discussion of the worth of sampling has been formulated in terms of E M V or expected monetary value. A particular survey may prove in reality to be more or less reliable than was expected before the research was carried out. The probabilities on the market share levels may therefore be different in some particular case which will affect the monetary amounts gained from carrying out the survey. This means that the actual gain from sample information will generally differ from that expected initially, even though in the long run actual gains will total expected gains. Nevertheless the concept of expectation gives the marketing manager the best economic indication of the worth of various possible survey options before they are carried out and avoids the dangers of the 'seat of the pants' type of approach.

A decision tree is not a panacea. Like any other management technique, it can be misused, and has some special dangers of its own. Firstly, the tree itself requires skilful construction to ensure that it is not over-complex but adequately represents the correct problem. Managers who understand decision trees find the logic an excellent way of clearing their minds on relationships and options, and of laying bare the underlying structure of a problem in a way which forces all the feasible alternatives to be looked at, and contingency plans to be made. Alternatives which have been ignored, or possibilities of a reversal demanding a contingency plan, are more easily exposed. Setting up all but the very simplest trees usually needs the help of skilled experts.

To analyse a tree the relevant information must be determined, quantified, and assembled. While there appear to be well-understood and accepted procedures for dealing with cost and revenue data, this is not true of estimates of uncertainty. In most business decisions much of the information concerning uncertainty cannot be converted mechanically into probability estimates, so that the door is commonly left ajar to emotion, off-hand judgements, etc. The decision tree forces the actual estimates made to be written down for each separate portion of the tree and to be seen, discussed, and challenged by others.

Coping with Risk

Decision trees help to cope with risk, but they do not eliminate it. No matter how well the probabilities and payoffs have been estimated and how well the tree has been structured and analysed, things may turn out badly for the decision-maker. The decision taken may not produce as good a result as the one which would have been chosen with the benefit of hindsight. It is easy to be wise after the event; the kind of analysis outlined in this article aims to provide the best decision in the light of what is known at the time the decision is taken. By following the methods outlined, the success rate should, over a period, be raised. If organizations could raise their success rate even marginally, most of them would find that their profitability would increase out of all proportion to the relative changes.

Decision trees also allow the expertise of experts in different areas of knowledge and understanding to be brought together and combined into a single logical judgement. It is, of course, axiomatic that experts are often wrong. One of the important responsibilities of top management is to judge accurately the abilities of the experts they use. The decision analysis approach allows experts to give expression to their doubts as well as to their opinions. Such information is valuable and can be properly used, so that, over a period of time, an expert can be judged, not just by the occasions on which he was right or wrong, but also by how his forecasts compare with the range of probabilities that he has given. In this situation his biases can be calibrated. In many instances when an expert makes inaccurate estimates the error arises from assumptions, which he is forced to make, on topics which are in essence nothing to do with the expert's professional field. A decision tree allows management to use an expert within his own professional field, which is fairer to the experts concerned and more useful to management.

Managers and management techniques can only be asked to do as well as is possible in the circumstances. Judged by this criterion, decision analysis is a powerful, general, and flexible tool. It is perhaps a measure of the applicability of the methods that both the companies using the technique and the areas of application have been growing rapidly in recent years. Areas in which decision analysis techniques have been successfully applied by organizations as disparate as Unilever and the Civil Aviation Authority, a finance company and an engineering consortium are: investment decisions – new plant, etc.; decisions on when, and in what form, new products should be launched; choice of the

27

optimum level of a market research investigation; choice of a suitable flight data processing system for development; oil and gas exploration decisions; pricing decisions for a product in a competitive and uncertain environment; competitive bidding decisions; quality control decisions – but the areas to which these techniques could be applied are virtually limitless.

Many managers still feel uncomfortable about the use of decision trees. This is probably because they find themselves being forced to think in an uncomfortable mould and to lay bare to analysts some of the more delicate considerations which enter into their personal approach to decision-making. Such considerations may include confidential information, admissions of uncertainty (running contrary to the accepted views of managerial culture) and embarrassing motivations (such as wanting a European subsidiary to be located near the International School at Geneva for their own children). The advantages are, however, generally accepted as being fourfold: (1) focusing of both formal and informal thinking on the critical issues; (2) forcing into the open assumptions which would otherwise remain hidden; (3) gain in consistency and coherence in decision-making; (4) effectiveness in communicating the reasoning which underlies the decision to all those concerned with the implementation.

2 Harman Merchants Ltd: A Reorganization
(Written as at early 1973)

Introduction

The following case study provides an expansive illustration of a situation facing the holding company of a large industrial group early in 1973. The parent company, known as Harman Merchants Ltd, was confronted with the urgent need to reorganize some of its subsidiaries in order that they might benefit more widely from their participation in a group-structure form of organization. Three subsidiaries in particular were chosen for detailed investigation, and all three were located in or around the Scunthorpe area. Significantly, general industrial and commercial forecasts had predicted that the Scunthorpe area would be one of above average growth and heavy expansion, and thus the parent company wanted to ensure that, together with its subsidiaries, it would be able to benefit from the anticipated growth.

Harman Merchants' main activity was in the field of building and plumbing, and much of its early growth had been achieved by the acquisition of small companies within allied areas of production. The three subsidiaries mentioned above were examples of such acquisitions. In 1964 Harman Merchants had taken over a traditional firm of builders merchants, based in Scunthorpe and known as Harold Jones & Co. Ltd. Although cautious in the early years of its expansionary policy, encouraging sales results prompted the parent company to increase its rate of growth. By 1967 the company was increasingly confident of its ability to thrive on a wider scale of business activity and the rate of expansion became rapid, with heavy involvement in building merchants' firms throughout the south and east of England. In 1970 Harman Merchants acquired the second of its subsidiaries in Scunthorpe: a glass merchants called Denbys. Two years later it took over a Scunthorpe-based firm of heating suppliers and architectural ironmongers named Baileys.

In terms of turnover during the years between 1967 and 1973, there was an increase from £1,000,000 to over £5,000,000. The pre-tax profits rose from £50,000 to over £300,000. The breakdown according to activity for 1972 is given in Appendix 1.

Before defining the problem more specifically, it seems relevant at this stage to outline the main activities of the individual subsidiaries under investigation, and to look at each firm in relation to their sales, capital assets, and available work force.

Harold Jones & Co. Ltd

The earliest acquisition was Harold Jones & Co. Ltd. The company's prime interest lay in the supply of domestic boilers, standard sanitary fittings (rather than luxury models), gutters, down pipes, etc., iron and copper tubes and fittings, brass ware, and water tanks. Traditionally the firm was strong in Lincolnshire, and its area of business encompassed markets as far south as Spalding and Peterborough. At the same time, deliveries were also made as far north as Wetherby in Yorkshire. However, the amount of business done in Scunthorpe was comparatively weak.

The majority of its sales were made to firms of plumbers. It supplied both the sole trader and the large-scale business, and also provided local councils with equipment. The amount of transactions performed in this latter category amounted to about 15 per cent of total turnover. In addition to these outlets, about 9 per cent of the total sales were through direct selling, that is, directly from the factory to the customer. The firm had no showroom facilities, and the proportion of retail trade involved was comparatively low: approximately 8 per cent of total trade. Although lacking in showroom facilities, the amount of business done at the trade counter was very high and such sales formed a large part of the deliveries made. Indeed, approximately 85 per cent of all sales were subsequently delivered by the company.

The buildings used by the firm were owned freehold. They not only tended to be old and in need of repair, but were also rather cramped in view of the high stock turnover. It was generally agreed that the buildings were used to full capacity and that there was a strong tendency for heavy congestion within the available storage space; moreover it was recognized that any possible increase in sales would be necessarily limited by the continual problem of saturated storage capacity. Hence it was felt that any

30

increase in sales would have to be dealt with through direct selling methods. Whilst the total amount of available space was 10,000 square feet, it was estimated that any long-term expansion would necessitate at least double the accessible amount of space.

Forty people were employed by Harold Jones & Co. Ltd, and four delivery vehicles were maintained.

Denbys Ltd

The second acquisition from within the Scunthorpe area was the purchase of a controlling interest in a firm of glass merchants called Denbys Ltd. The firm occupied an old, two-storey building on the outskirts of the town. The building was rented from the town council at what was generally considered to be a nominal fee. The main trading functions of the firm revolved around glass, and Denbys' principal activity was to cut to size the glass, which had been delivered by Pilkingtons, and subsequently to deliver the cut glass to customers.

85 per cent of all sales were to trade, 70 per cent of sales being for new housing work and about 15 per cent for double-glazing. Additional contracts were held with two greenhouse manufacturers known as Maidstone and Cranebridge, and these two contracts entailed supplying greenhouse glass for domestic greenhouses in the South Humberside region. This work accounted for about 12 per cent of sales. As regards the proportion of sales delivered to customers by Denbys, this was generally about 90 per cent of total sales.

The rented accommodation was used for both warehouse and office purposes. Although the cost of the accommodation was minimal, it was not very suitable for its main function, that is for the storage of glass. Firstly, the access height was not sufficient to accommodate readily the larger sizes of float glass delivered by Pilkingtons, and there was also inadequate space available to allow for the installation of overhead lifting gear. Hence the operations of loading and unloading delivery lorries became a very time-consuming occupation. Furthermore the contract with Pilkingtons contained a penalty clause, should any delays be incurred by delivery lorries, and thus Denbys were under constant pressure to maintain a very strict time schedule.

The firm's offices were attached to the warehouse and, although the entrance area provided a small space to set up displays, samples, etc., the general surroundings of the site were most unexciting and unlikely to stimulate much interest for a developing retail trade.

The total staff employed numbered thirteen, and three delivery vehicles were available for company use.

Baileys Ltd

Located in the commercial centre of Scunthorpe, the sales organization of Baileys was divided into a number of specialist divisions. These included departments for architectural brassware, heating, tools, and sanitary ware.

Historically Baileys had earned an excellent reputation for both their standard of service and their ability to supply virtually anything from stock. However, a combination of mismanagement and general neglect had eroded the long-established goodwill. Fortunately sales forecasts pointed to a likely improvement in trade, and the firm seemed to be on the verge of regaining some of its former profitability.

The areas serviced by Baileys ranged over the whole of the Humberside region, with excellent trading results there when compared with those achieved in the Lincolnshire district. Approximately 9 per cent of total sales were to retail customers, and about a quarter of these sales were collected by the purchasers rather than delivered.

As stated, the two-acre site was situated in the commercial centre of the city, but its layout was not very suitable for its principal usage. The main building was very old and rambling, and was built on many levels. Furthermore it also formed part of a complex which contained a scheduled historic building in the form of a school. In addition the block contained council-owned offices. As regards the general accessibility of the building, this was poor. Large vehicles had great difficulty in gaining access, as the site was bounded on three sides by very narrow streets, and on the fourth side access was completely prohibited. The streets to the east, west and south were exceptionally narrow, whilst the road on the north boundary, called Watergate, formed part of a new ring-road, to which Baileys would not have direct access.

At the time of the take-over, the number of staff employed

by Baileys was eighty. However this was gradually reduced, and in early 1973 it numbered fifty. Five delivery vehicles were owned. Appendix 2 summarizes the financial statements of the three subsidiaries for 1972.

Harman Merchants' 1973 Problem

It was in the early part of 1973 that Ian Pearson, Chairman of the parent company, recognized the urgent necessity for the reorganization of these three Scunthorpe subsidiaries. Ian Pearson believed that any analysis of the current and future situation would be enriched by the expertise to be offered by a specialist in decision analysis, and for this reason invited Peter Hopper to act as a consultant to the group.

Peter Hopper immediately reported that the most basic need common to all three subsidiaries was for new premises. Although Denbys could possibly have rebuilt on their existing site, it was felt that there would be little geographical advantage in so doing. Similarly Jones and Baileys could have rebuilt, but such a decision would cause massive disruption of their trading, and would be a highly unpopular choice. Another alternative would be to amalgamate either all three firms on to one site, or at least to amalgamate Jones and Baileys. Although amalgamation of all three was a possible solution, it was felt that this was a less realistic choice, largely because Denbys' business was very different in nature from that of the other subsidiaries.

Since a variety of viable alternative strategies existed, it was decided to set out the relative advantages and disadvantages of both rebuilding and/or amalgamation. These are shown in Appendix 3.

It was also agreed to study the market for builders merchants' goods within the area in terms of expected trends, and to look at the general development of the Scunthorpe district in terms of accessibility, communications, etc.

To assist in the assessment of the likely changes in the market, it was decided to consult a paper published by the Building and Civil Engineering Economic Development Council (which formed part of the National Economic Development Office), entitled 'Regional Forecasting for Construction in Yorkshire and Humberside'. This pilot study predicted an above-average growth rate in construction of 4·5 per cent per annum in real terms, which was well above the average predicted for the whole country. Contributory factors in this forecast included Humberside's designation as an intermediate development area; the Humber Bridge project, which was due to start in 1973 with a completion date of 1976; the increasing accessibility of Scunthorpe achieved by the linkage of the M1 and M62 via the M18. However, it was also recognized that, whilst Scunthorpe became more accessible, at the same time it would become implicitly more attractive as a base for other builders merchants. There already existed one very strong competitor in that area, namely United Builders Merchants, and evidence suggested that another company, Kennedys, was considering moving their base to the district.

In terms of the likely changes in Scunthorpe, one of the most important within the Scunthorpe area, already described, was the development of the new north ring-road, which circumvented the Baileys site. At the time of the investigation this road was the only one in the process of being built, and in practical terms it meant that the area surrounding Baileys was likely to become far more highly developed as a shopping and commercial centre. Such development had been anticipated to a large extent, and the old market-place had already been cleared away and plans passed for the site to be used for a supermarket, multi-storey car park, and Trust House Hotel. The development of a new pedestrian precinct within the area had also played a part in encouraging a shift in the location of the shopping centre. Finally, the local council had manifested its strong interest in the possibility of sponsoring large redevelopment in that area, mainly by enforcing compulsory purchase orders upon a number of buildings near to the site.

In view of the above comments it seemed valid to assume that Baileys would be a valuable site for redevelopment as offices and shops but not for reorganization as a builders merchants' site. However, it was recognized that this high site value might not be fully realized until the redevelopment of the area became more apparent. In addition it was important to take into account the fact that part of the block was a scheduled historic building, and that part of the building was already occupied by a council office.

As far as the two other buildings were concerned, then, the

anticipated changes in Scunthorpe would affect Harold Jones's building only to the extent that it might have site value rather than intrinsic worth. Given the expected extensive redevelopment, it might be assumed that the site value would obviously increase, but it was also agreed that the site would not have the same potential as could be assigned to Baileys'. Little discussion was necessary regarding Denbys as the site was rented from the council and thus it had no redevelopment value as such for the tenant.

The Alternative Strategies

Peter Hopper recognized that a large number of alternative strategies could exist by simply permutating (i) rebuilding site, (ii) which companies would amalgamate and (iii) when a site could be rebuilt. He decided to reduce the number of alternatives to a workable group, which could then be analysed in a logical framework. Lengthy discussions with various members of the appropriate companies resulted in the elimination of most of the alternatives, and it is useful to look at certain key issues in this process of elimination.

The first area which Peter Hopper thought it crucial to study was the problem of the site location. It was widely agreed that none of the existing sites provided any readily adaptable specifications for rebuilding to be a viable proposition. It was accepted that the most suitable site accommodation would be a single-storey warehouse which could offer ample space for later expansion. Of the three existing sites only one was large enough to accommodate the possible amalgamation of the three subsidiaries, namely Baileys. However, as Baileys was located in the centre of the town, it was considered to be far too valuable for any such development, and in addition it was considered highly unlikely that planning permission would be granted. This analysis was accepted without argument, and it was then suggested that a more suitable site might be found to the east of Scunthorpe, thereby making use of new roads planned for the Humber Bridge and Scunthorpe district. The second and cheaper option was to move to a new development area, known as the Lynas Industrial Estate, which was located to the south of the planned Scunthorpe by-pass.

As regards the choice of when any new development might take place, it was agreed that, even if a decision was made immediately, there would have to be a time lag of at least six months to allow for planning, and a possible additional twelve-month period for the building work. Given such constraints, the earliest date on which a new building could be opened would be January 1975. Seen from another perspective, the argument was raised that it might be more prudent to delay any decision until the Humber Bridge project had been completed, thereby obtaining some insight into the likely effectiveness of the improved communications system. If this strategy was adopted, then it implied a decision in mid-1976, followed by a possible opening date of January 1978. As a further possibility it was suggested that a compromise decision could be delayed until the end of 1974, with a subsequent move in July 1976, which could coincide with the Bridge opening.

Regarding the decision as to which of the subsidiaries should be amalgamated, it was recognized that, of the three companies, Baileys and Jones were the more similar in general terms. Thus these two subsidiaries seemed more adaptable to possible amalgamation than did any other combination. However, if an immediate decision were to be taken, it was thought it might be sensible to amalgamate all three on to one site in order to minimize potential building costs. At the same time as these discussions occurred, the internal management within Denbys felt that it would be advantageous to draw up their plans for development, and had gone ahead and done so. Given that this potential redevelopment might occur, it also seemed sensible to acquire sufficient land to facilitate a later move by Baileys and Jones, should the decision be taken to place all subsidiaries on a common site.

As a result, seven strategies now remained:

(i) Maintain the *status quo*.
(ii) Build new accommodation for Denbys in anticipation of a possible move towards the latter part of July 1974.
(iii) Move all three subsidiaries in July 1975.
(iv) Rebuild as in (iii) but move during July 1976.
(v) Relocate Denbys and move during late 1974, consolidating

the move with additional building to accommodate Jones and Baileys in July 1976.

(vi) Transfer all subsidiaries to new accommodation during January 1978.

(vii) Relocate Denby during the latter part of 1974, simultaneously postponing any move by Jones and Baileys until January 1978.

Strategies (iii)–(vii) inclusive also involved a choice of site, that is, of south or east Scunthorpe.

Assessing the Uncertainties

Although the number of potential strategies was narrowed down to the range given above it was, at the same time, recognized that the problem of choosing between the sites was exacerbated by the awareness that the outcome of events anticipated to occur between 1973–8 might well effect which strategy was optimal. Peter Hopper pointed out that, if these uncertain events could be quantified explicitly, then the problem of choosing between the strategies could be analysed by using a decision tree.

It was agreed that five basic areas of uncertainty existed. These were:

(i) Likely growth in the overall market for building materials on the South Humberside.

(ii) Possible growth of competition.

(iii) To what extent the value of Baileys site might change.

(iv) How rapid the progress of the bridge- and road-building programme would be.

(v) How the gross profit margin was likely to change.

After lengthy discussions with managerial staff in Scunthorpe, Peter Hopper concluded that two of these issues were crucial to any final decision. Firstly, it was very important to look at the overall potential growth of sales under different strategies (i) and, secondly, it was essential to have a guide to the likely change in value, with time, of Baileys' site (iii). Although profit margins were somewhat uncertain, it was felt that the historical trend could be extrapolated with a reasonable degree of confidence. It was obvious that a drop in sales would increase costs as a percentage of sales at fixed costs could not be reduced in the short run. However, subjective probability assessments indicated favourable sales figures even under pessimistic assumptions, and thus it was agreed not to include this sphere as a major uncertainty.

Subjective probability estimates of these two crucial uncertainties were obtained from the three general managers in Scunthorpe. Mr Hopper asked each manager to consider a pair of bets. One of these bets would be to choose a ball at random from an urn containing a known proportion of red and black balls; choosing a red ball wins. The other bet involved predicting that, say, Jones' sales would increase by at least x per cent per annum on average for the ensuing seven years.

By altering either the percentage of red and black balls, or the value of x, Mr Hopper was able to obtain cumulative distribution functions (CDF) for these uncertain events. Appendix 4 describes the procedure used.

By taking the $12\frac{1}{2}$, 50, and $87\frac{1}{2}$ percentiles of each distribution, the continuous distributions could be approximated by using a triple chance fork, with respective probabilities of $\frac{1}{4}$, $\frac{1}{2}$, and $\frac{1}{4}$ as shown in Figure 2.1. The results of these probability assessments are illustrated in Appendix 5.

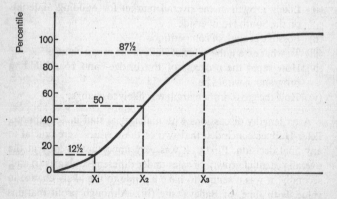

Figure 2.1 Obtaining the High-Medium-Low ($\frac{1}{4}$, $\frac{1}{2}$, $\frac{1}{4}$) Estimates from the Cumulative Distribution Function

Cost Estimation

In order to decide between the various strategies, Peter Hopper used the Net Present Value (NPV) of the cash flows resulting from that strategy. The way the cash flows were estimated was as follows:

(a) Take the sales estimates for that year or, if a move is involved in that year, for the parts of the year before and after the move.

(b) Deduct a percentage (2 per cent was used), if the original sales figure assumed a site in East Scunthorpe, in order to obtain likely sales in South Scunthorpe.

(c) Deduct a figure to represent collect-sales lost during the first two years of operation on a new site. This was taken as half the collect sales in year one and a quarter in year two, based on the estimated fraction of collect-sales in 1972–3.

(d) Estimate the: (1) gross margin
　　　　　　　　　(2) cost of selling,

using an amalgamation of: (1) historic trends (including other Harman operations)
　　　　　　　　　　　　　(2) management estimates
　　　　　　　　　　　　　(3) National Federation of Builders and Plumbers Merchants data.

(e) Derive the profit before interest and tax.

(f) Estimate the depreciation allowable for tax. (This is not very large, as there is comparatively little investment in plant and machinery. In addition, as the firms are in the distribution industry, regional grants are not available.)

(g) Estimate the increased working capital necessary to support the increase in sales (again by using the evidence available under (d) above).

(h) Hence, assuming a 50-per-cent corporation tax (Advanced Corporation Tax and Mainstream Tax) payable on average a year in arrears, the annual cash flow from operations was obtained as follows:

r = discount rate

S_t = sales in year t

a_t = gross margin in year t

c_t = selling cost in year t (dependent on sales growth)

ΔWC_t = increase in working capital in year t

D_t = depreciation for tax purposes in year t.

Cash flow from operations in year t is:

$$X_t = [S_t\,(a_t-c_t)-D_t]\left[1-\frac{0\cdot5}{(1+r)}\right]+D_t-\Delta WC_t$$

Cash flow from capital transactions (buying and selling land and buildings, etc.) is Y_t in year t.

Terminal value of fixed assets $= F_T$

Initial value of Working Capital $= WC_0$

Final value of working capital $= WC_0 + \sum\limits_{t=1}^{T} \Delta WC_t$

Hence, discounting at r per cent.

$$\text{NPV} = \sum_{t=1}^{T}\left\{\frac{(X_t+Y_t)}{(1+r)^t}\right\}+\frac{F_T+WC_0+\sum\limits_{t=1}^{T}\Delta WC_t}{(1+r)^T}$$

Notes on the actual costs used are shown in Appendix 6. From these cash flows Peter Hopper tabulated the NPVs of the various strategies (Appendix 7). He used an after-tax cost of capital of 13 per cent as the discount rate. The terminal date was 1980, as Peter Hopper felt that any transient effects due to the move would have evened out by then.

He also decided to use an expected-value criterion for choosing between strategies, since the Scunthorpe operations were only a small part of Harman Merchants Ltd and Mr Pearson estimated that Harman's were risk neutral for this size of investment.

Peter Hopper decided that the base value from which to compare NPVs should not be zero (as for conventional projects) but the amount of money that could be obtained at the present time by selling the three subsidiaries to a competitor. Estimates for this figure ranged from a high of £600,000 to a low of £450,000, the book value.

Issues for Discussion

What would you advise Harman's to do? How critical are the assigned probabilities to the particular recommendation?

Appendix 1 Harman Merchants Ltd
Performance in 1972 of the Three Divisions

	Turnover	Profits before interest and tax
1. Builders and Plumbers Merchants	59%	41%
2. Architectural Ironmongery	26%	30%
3. Industrial Heating Equipment	15%	29%

Appendix 2 Summarized Financial Statement of the Scunthorpe Subsidiaries (1972)

	Baileys (£000)	Jones (£000)	Denbys (£000)
Sales	490	550	109
Gross profit	109	90	34
less: Total expenditure	72	65	25
Net operating profit	37	25	9
less: Interest	3	0	0
Profit before tax	34	25	9
Fixed Assets	100	30	2
Debtors	90	100	20
Stocks	70	65	15
Creditors	50	60	15
Average net assets	190	130	25
Return on net assets (net operating profit/net assets)	19·5%	19·2%	36%
Stock turnover	7·0%	12·2%	7·3%
Debtors' turnover (months)	2·2	2·1	2·2
Salaries (as % of sales)	10·2%	7·2%	9%
Gross margin	22%	16%	31%

Appendix 3 Relative Advantages of Rebuilding/Amalgamation

(B J D refer to the three subsidiaries)

Advantages of Rebuilding

1. Less maintenance (B J D).
2. Better stock control, stock handling, etc. (B J D).
3. Can cope with increased demand (B J D).
4. Access height advantages (D).
5. Easier access to buildings (B J).

Disadvantages

1. Higher rent (D, and B J if not on own land).
2. Loss of some retail and collect trade (if on new site).

Advantages of Amalgamation

1. Slight saving in transport costs – combined deliveries, etc.
2. Saving in warehousemen/office staff through common stocks, stock control, accounting, etc.
3. Reduction in stocks that were held in common.
4. Improved management – one manager to coordinate all Harman's subsidiaries in Scunthorpe. This is perhaps the major advantage of amalgamation.

Disadvantage

1. Loss of corporate identity, effect on morale, etc.

Appendix 4 Example of Probability Assessment Procedure

Subjective probability assessments for the sales-growth rate were obtained directly to give the Cumulative Distribution Function.

The method used was to present the assessors with two fictitious bets and to alter the bets to obtain indifference between the two. The following diagram illustrates the procedure:

MR HOPPER: Imagine there is an opaque jar containing fifty red and fifty black balls. You are to choose one ball, without looking in the jar. If you choose a black ball, then you win £200, a red ball will win you nothing. Let's call this 'bet number 1'.

Now there's another bet in which you must consider the annual growth rate of X's sales over the next seven years assuming they carry on trading in the same line of business and from the same premises.

This second bet is as follows: if X's sales growth exceeds 11 per cent per annum, you win £200, if not, you win nothing. These two bets can be illustrated thus:

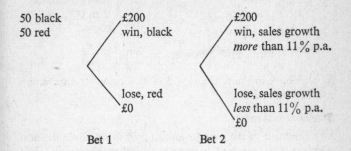

50 black
50 red

£200
win, black

lose, red
£0

Bet 1

£200
win, sales growth *more* than 11% p.a.

lose, sales growth *less* than 11% p.a.
£0

Bet 2

Which bet do you prefer?

ASSESSOR: I think I'd go for bet 1, 11 per cent seems a bit steep.
MR HOPPER: Imagine then a new choice.

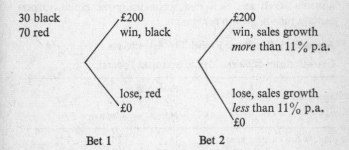

30 black
70 red

£200
win, black

lose, red
£0

Bet 1

£200
win, sales growth *more* than 11% p.a.

lose, sales growth *less* than 11% p.a.
£0

Bet 2

ASSESSOR: Well this time bet 2 seems a better choice.

Eventually, by altering either the number of red and black balls, or the percentage growth rate, a point can be achieved where the assessor is 'indifferent' – he cannot choose between the two bets.

In this way a cumulative distribution function can be obtained since when:

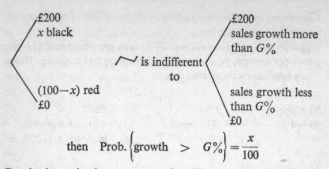

$$\text{then} \quad \text{Prob.} \left\{\text{growth} \; > \; G\%\right\} = \frac{x}{100}$$

By altering x in the range, say, $5 \to 95$ a complete distribution could be obtained.

Note on growth rates

An assessment of the average annual growth rate over the next seven years was required. In practice a number of assessors found it difficult to think in terms of percentage growth *rates*, so tables were prepared which translated growth rates into sales on an annual basis. The assessor was then asked to consider the £-sales amount in five years' time. The CDF was then prepared as before and the x-axis was converted, again using the tables, to percentage rates of growth per annum.

Appendix 5 Results of Probability Assessments

Growth Rates of Sales, % (p.a. over next 7 years)

| | Probabilities | | |
| | 0·25 | 0·5 | 0·25 |
	High	Medium	Low
Baileys (on existing site)	16%	12%	7%
Jones (on existing site)	11%	9%	7%
Denbys (on existing site)	14%	10%	6½%
Denbys (on new site)	20%	16%	12½%
Baileys and Jones (on new site)	18%	13½%	9%
Baileys' value			
January 1975	£150,000	£110,000	£90,000
July 1976	£180,000	£140,000	£100,000
January 1978	£220,000	£160,000	£120,000

Conditional assessments

In assessing Baileys' value, it was assumed that a valuation of Baileys would be undertaken at three points in time, January 1975, July 1976, and January 1978. The CDF of each of these valuations was required. However, there was a further problem in that if, say, a high valuation resulted in 1975, a high valuation was *more* likely in 1976. In practice, managers found it very difficult to think about conditional probabilities, and only a small allowance was made for them as they did not appear to affect the overall analysis significantly. For example, if a high value occurred in 1976, the probability of a high value in 1978 was put at 0·3 (not 0·25) and a low value was put at 0·2 (not 0·25). Similarly for a low value, following a low value the probability was put at 0·3 and for a high value following a low value it was put at 0·2. These differences were found not to affect the analysis significantly.

Appendix 6 Peter Hopper's Notes on Cash-Flow Estimates

(i) Baileys' value has been treated separately in Appendix 8.
(ii) Jones's building is assumed to have a value of:
    £35,000 in January 1975
    £40,000 in July 1976
    £46,000 in January 1978
    £60,000 in December 1979.
(iii) Working capital is valued at balance sheet prices. It has been found that at Norwich working capital has increased as 14 per cent of sales. This figure was used in the analysis. (Norwich is Harman Merchants' most modern operation.)
(iv) Depreciation was taken as a percentage of sales (though of course in the short run it would be fixed).
    Depreciation: 0·4% of sales at Denbys
                  0·7% of sales at Baileys
                  0·3% of sales at Jones
                  0·4% of sales at the new site.

(This last figure is obviously higher in the first year after the move, since 100-per-cent write-off is allowed on certain items.)

(v) Profit margins

	1972–3			1968–9	1969–70	1970–71	1971–2	1972–73
	Baileys	Jones	Denbys	Harman Merchants (Norwich)				
Sales (actual) £000	490	550	109					
Sales (on a percentage base)	100	100	100	100	100	100	100	100
Gross profit (on a percentage base)	22	16	31 *	15·6	15·7	15·2	15·8	16·2
Costs (on a percentage base)	14·5	11·4	22·8	13·0	13·5	13·4	13·3	12·0
Net profit (on a percentage base)	7·5	4·6	8·2	2·6	2·2	1·8	2·5	4·2

* The gross margin of Denbys in 1972–3 was abnormally high due to a price rise affecting existing stocks.

It is felt that, as in the past, the trend will be towards lower gross margins, but Harman Merchants' increasing size will give it the buying power to help counteract this trend.

There will be an initial gradual improvement in selling costs irrespective of any move, but in the absence of a move it is felt costs will rise again in the late 1970s due to wage inflation.

At the move, a sharp drop in costs should occur as the economies of a combined operation under one roof, which were mentioned previously, are achieved. It is hoped that the move at Scunthorpe could prove instructive and keep the costs of moving to a minimum. The temporary loss of part of the collect-trade is, however, virtually inevitable.

(vi) The value of the business at the end of the seven-year period analysed is taken to be merely the building value plus working capital.

(vii) *New building*

    (1) Costs increase at 6 per cent p.a.

    (2) Present cost of single-frame, specially built warehouse is £4·25 per square foot.

    Required for Baileys and Jones.

(a) Baileys at present have 75,000 square feet, but in a *suitable building* could only need about 35,000 square feet.

(b) Harold Jones have 10,300 square feet but could use more at present and should thus allow for 20,000 square feet in a new building.

This implies a new building of say 60,000 square feet including office accommodation.

With Denbys an extra 10,000 square feet may be needed, including an entrance height sufficient for the large sizes of float glass.

Obviously it would be more expensive to build a separate building for Denbys unless the height differential proved difficult to overcome.

The land cost varies considerably between South Scunthorpe (e.g. Lynas Estate) and East Scunthorpe (British Rail land). Annual Rent (reviewable every five years).

(i) South Scunthorpe £1,500 per acre.

(ii) East Scunthorpe £2,500 per acre.

About four acres would be required. It may be possible to obtain a 999-year lease.

New building costs

(1) Jones and Baileys and Denbys
70,000 square feet at £4·25 or £298,000

(2) Jones and Baileys, Denbys separate, would cost an additional £10,000. (Rate higher than £4·25 for small building.)

(3) Land – South Scunthorpe £6,000 p.a.
East Scunthorpe £10,000 p.a.
(assume rising to £10,000 not £14,000 p.a. after five years).

(4) Fixtures and fittings taken as £30,000.

Appendix 7

* Net Present Value of Alternative Strategies

Strategy	Market growth	Site	NPV_I	NPV_{II}	TOTAL NPV
Status quo	High		290	281	571
	Medium		279	250	529
	Low		258	205	463
Denbys build,	High		289	250	539
move late 1974	Medium		290	219	509
	Low		295	174	469
Jones and Baileys	High	East	395	211	606
and Denbys		South	387	228	615
build, move	Medium	East	380	149	529
January 1975		South	373	165	538
	Low	East	371	98	469
		South	365	115	480
Jones, Baileys	High	East	349	219	568
and Denbys build,		South	345	235	580
move July 1976	Medium	East	340	171	511
		South	336	187	523
	Low	East	334	120	454
		South	331	136	467
Denbys build,	High	East	356	212	568
moving late 1974		South	351	228	579
Jones and Baileys	Medium	East	344	163	507
move July 1976		South	339	179	518
	Low	East	345	112	457
		South	341	128	469
Jones, Baileys	High	East	313	214	527
and Denbys build,		South	310	230	540
moving January	Medium	East	308	168	476
1978		South	306	184	490
	Low	East	311	123	434
		South	309	139	448

NPV_I = NPV of cash flow from operations
NPV_{II} = NPV of capital cash flows, including terminal values
* A discount rate of 13 per cent was used, as this was the best estimate of Harman's opportunity cost of capital for this project.

NPV of Alternative Strategies (contd)

Strategy	Market growth	Site	NPV_I	NPV_{II}	TOTAL NPV
Denbys build	High	East	318	222	540
mainly late 1974		South	315	239	554
Jones and Baileys	Medium	East	310	177	487
build, moving		South	308	193	501
January 1978	Low	East	317	130	447
		South	316	146	462

Appendix 8

NPV of Baileys' Sale Value
(£000)

| | January 1975 | | | July 1976 | | | January 1978 | | | |
	High	Medium	Low	High	Medium	Low	High	Medium	Low	Terminal
Actual	150	110	90	180	140	100	220	160	120	200
NPV	121	89	73	121	96	67	123	90	67	85

3 The Introduction of an Automatic Landing System in Limited Visibility Conditions
(Written as at 1968)

The economics of civil aviation in Europe depend on the ability to compete with alternative transport; for short-stage flights this means that scheduled airlines must be able to operate to a time-table and in all weather conditions. During the 1960s the British aircraft industry accordingly initiated development of automatic landing systems for its new civil aircraft. These systems would facilitate the safe landing of aircraft in weather conditions of more limited visibility than at present, and were to be introduced by 1971. For world-wide use, such systems were to use the inter-national standard landing guidance systems referred to as ILS (Instrument Landing System), but required a more accurate and reliable version.

Concurrently, the National Air Traffic Services (NATS) were in the process of introducing such a version of ILS and were successful in achieving world-wide adoption of its standards and characteristics; it was to be called a 'Category III' ILS and made available by 1971. During 1968, however, contrary advice was received from a scientific establishment working on the develop-ment of automatic landing and related navigational systems. It was believed that extraneous radio interference would present too great a threat to the safe operation of Category III ILS to permit civil operations at the acceptable standards of safety in the low visibility conditions contemplated. NATS thus had to make a primary decision whether to continue the introduction of Category III ILS.

The circumstances, however, were such that in 1968 NATS had gone ahead with the Category III ILS and this decision could not be reversed. The airlines were committed to a three-year programme to fit aircraft with the appropriate equipment and, from 1971, any delay in the availability of a suitable landing guidance system could be considered as equivalent to incurring a cost of £½m. per year. The additional benefit to the UK air transport industry of a usable Category III system was also evaluated using a monetary criterion: £1m. per year; while the cost of proceeding with the Category III ILS was estimated at £2·5 m. Because not enough was known, either of the incidence of extraneous interference or of the ability of the airborne equipment and flight control systems to perform correctly in its presence, an assessment was made as to whether the scientific advice was true fact. It was believed that there was only a 0·55 probability that the Category III ILS system would, in 1971, be found to give acceptable standards of safety.

The same scientific establishment suggested the development of an 'Environmental Monitor' (EM), which, by detecting and warning of the presence of extraneous interference, could be used to ensure that the landing system safety was never compromised. The pilots were warned to overshoot whenever there was risk. This suggestion then presented a second alternative: namely whether to request development of an EM, concurrently with going ahead with the Category III ILS. Development of the EM would cost £1m. and was expected to take three years. If, by 1971, any lack of integrity was discovered in the use of Category III ILS, the successful development of an EM would, without doubt, be effective in overcoming it. NATS assessed a 0·75 probability that such a development would be successful. Of course, it may well be that the expenditure would be unproductive in the event that ILS alone performs successfully. This option to develop would still exist if the worst fears on the reliability of the Category III ILS were later realized; it would just have been delayed three years. If neither the development of an EM nor the Category III ILS were successful, the automatic landing project would effectively collapse.

A third option also emerged: to commission a one-year intensive study and simulation by an aircraft manufacturer into the ability of the aircraft equipment to operate properly in the presence of extraneous interference. NATS assessed the probability that this study would show that the aircraft equipment was likely to operate properly as 0·6 and the probability that it would be found vulnerable therefore as 0·4. In the former case the additional encouraging evidence would permit re-assessment of the probability of the correctness of the scientific advice on the Category III ILS, namely that it would not operate successfully, downwards from 0·45 to 0·35, in the latter case upwards to 0·6. The £½m. study would not, however, yield any additional information with relation to the probably successful development of the EM. The benefits of further knowledge about the external interference had to be traded off against the one year delay and thus also the earliest availability of the Environmental Monitor, should it be developed, which would then be 1972.

NATS decided to adopt a decision analysis approach. In order to be able to consider the problem, simplifying assumptions were made concerning the value of the money payoffs over time. Firstly, the likely volume of air traffic, and therefore the total benefits from a Category III landing system over the thirteen-year time horizon to 1981 was assumed to be increasing, and at such a rate as to wholly offset the discounting factor strictly necessary to compare today the worth of a sum of money to be obtained in future years. Secondly, it was agreed that profits and losses after 1981 should be ignored since ground and airline re-equipment would be necessary by that time.

Issues for Discussion

Using the information available to NATS and its assessment of probabilities, construct a decision tree from 1968 and indicate a course of action. How sensitive is this decision to the initial assessment of the correctness of the advice received in 1968?

Acknowledgement

The kind cooperation of Mr R. E. Cox, Director of Telecommunications (Communications and Navigation) and Mr M. Whitney, Deputy Director of Telecommunication (Navigation), in the formulation of this exercise is gratefully acknowledged.

4 Aeropa Ltd: A Financial Crossroads
(Written as at 1972)

General Background

Aeropa is a UK-based company engaged on the research, design, development, and production of civil and military aircraft. It employs about 16,000 workers in three different factories (at Accrington, Bawtry, and Cannock) and has an impressive record as a pioneer in a fiercely competitive high-risk industry.

The company's plans for the 1970s centre around the manufacture of three civil aircraft:

(i) Arrol – a highly successful short-hauler (215 sales to date) which first entered production six years ago and is now still being manufactured at Cannock.

(ii) Skylark – a government-sponsored long-hauler still in the research and development stage but scheduled to enter production in late 1974.

(iii) Stol – a new subsonic short-hauler which has not yet entered the research and development stage.

Market Forecasts

The Marketing Director, Dave Singer, has put forward the following notes on the market forecasts for the three aircraft.

(a) Arrol.
Sales of Arrol are declining fast. The potential future sales of the aircraft now depend critically on trade negotiations which will take place between Britain and Communist Bloc countries during the next twelve months. If a trade agreement is reached, Aeropa's market analysts estimate that the company will be able to make thirty further sales of the aircraft; on the other hand, if the negotiations fail, only ten further sales are expected. Some time ago the company employed a team of independent experts to evaluate the likely outcome of the negotiations. They came to the conclusion that 'although the outcome of trade negotiations is

53

never certain, there does seem to be an above-average chance of success in this case'.

(b) Skylark.

The company has less information on which to base sales forecasts for Skylark. Furthermore, the situation is complicated by there being a small chance that, sometime in the course of the next two years, the government will decide against the aircraft entering production at all.

If Skylark does enter production, and more than 150 sales are made, then it will be considered a success and further development work on the aircraft is certain to take place; on the other hand, if less than 150 sales are made, the aircraft will be deemed to be a failure and there is likely to be very little further development work. At present 'success' and 'failure' are considered to be equally likely.

(c) Stol.

The company's market analysts are reluctant to make any sales predictions for Stol at all. They do, however, all agree that a market for the aircraft will develop in about six years time (i.e. 1978) and consider that there is a high chance of this market being sufficiently large for Aeropa to wish to enter it.

The Current Situation

Aeropa is currently in serious financial difficulties which have built up over the past few months. At the centre of these difficulties is a £15m. loan which is due for repayment in three months' time. The Board have spent some time in searching for ways of handling the situation and have reached the view that they have only two options, namely:

(a) Close Cannock, so that enough money is released to repay the loan on time, or
(b) negotiate an extension to the loan.

Clearly the choice is a very important one; it will, to a large extent, determine the company's profitability and manufacturing capability in future years. The Board of Directors are divided on the issue. Some favour (a), others (b). At the moment Joe Purdy

(Production Director), Dave Singer (Marketing Director), Robert Knowles (Corporate Planning Director), and Geoff Franks (Finance Director) are having a tense discussion of the problem:

JOE: I favour closing the Cannock Plant so that we can repay the loan on time. I know that this means abandoning production of Arrol almost immediately, but surely that's to our advantage. The plant at Cannock is rapidly becoming severely under-utilized. Arrol will soon actually be making a loss if we keep it going. What's more, I can transfer production of Arrol's spares from Cannock to Bawtry without any difficulty.

DAVE: Yes, that's all very well as far as Arrol is concerned, but what about Skylark? I know that, because all the costs of development are paid for by the taxpayer, the government will take all the profit – if any – from the sales. But, nevertheless, we are committed to developing Skylark to the full and to producing as many as the market will bear. Now exploring the various options let us suppose that the market will bear 250. How would you then cope, Joe, with only two factories.

JOE: Don't worry. I've done some calculations on that already. When it became clear that sales were going to reach 250, I'd recruit another 3,000 operatives for Accrington and Bawtry. I know that sounds a lot but, Dave, you're assuming Skylark will be a success. If it's a failure I'd only have to recruit another 1,000 or so operatives. And don't forget, Skylark may never enter production. If that happens, we'll have no choice – we'll have to close both Accrington and Cannock.

ROBERT: Yes, I agree with you, Joe; if Skylark never enters production we have to contract. Still, for the time being, let us suppose we get the green light for Skylark. Suppose first that it is a failure, selling only 100. With two factories open, when would we be in a position to start manufacturing Stol?

JOE: 1979, I should say.

ROBERT: And if Skylark is successful, selling 250?

JOE: Well in that case I have to admit that Skylark would keep two factories busy for quite a long time. 1984 would be the earliest date for the production of Stol. But I'm not so sure about the value of planning so far ahead. You've admitted yourself, on occasion, that we may not even want to be in the Stol market.

ROBERT: I know that, but I think we've got to work on the assumption that we will want to be in it. We've got to take decisions now which will allow us to manufacture Stol in 1978 – not 1984. Now, if we negotiate an extension to this loan, three factories are kept open. Then, even if Skylark's a roaring success, we'll still have enough capacity to produce Stol in 1978. Of course if Skylark failed to enter production then we'd have to close two factories in 1974, but in that case, with no Skylark, we'd still have enough capacity to produce Stol in 1978.

GEOFF: I see your point Robert, but I don't think you've really considered how much all this is going to cost us. If Stol's development costs are excluded, then my department has shown that by closing Cannock now and repaying the loan we stand to make £6m. profit in the period 1972–8. Now that's not bad considering that Skylark, being government sponsored, makes no contribution to our profit. However, if we negotiate an extension to the loan, then the best that can happen is that the trade talks with the Communists succeed. We then make £1m. profit. If they fail, we incur enormous support costs at Cannock. The result? £10m. loss. Unthinkable!

DAVE: Surely it's not quite as bad as that. If the trade talks fail, then, in a year's time, we can reconsider our decision and maybe choose at that stage to close Cannock and repay the loan.

GEOFF: Yes, we've looked into that one as well. If we only negotiate an extension to the loan for one year in the first instance, then, if trade talks fail, we could still close Cannock and repay the loan. But in that case we'd lose £3m. in the period 1972–8. Delaying the decision costs us money.

ROBERT: I still think that the important thing is for us to be in as strong a position as possible to meet the demand for Skylark and Stol . . .

The Managing Director who has been listening to this discussion in silence is frankly worried. There ought, he feels, to be some systematic way of pooling the knowledge of Joe, Dave,

Robert, and Geoff so as to deal with the uncertainties. Unfortunately he does not know what it is.

He remembers, however, a business acquaintance of his who told him of the work of a consultant, Mr Wherton, who had helped to analyse a complex problem full of doubts and uncertainties concerning a possible plant expansion. He suggests to his colleagues that they should ask Mr Wherton along to work with them on the problem. The meeting readily agreed to this suggestion, provided that it would be treated as a matter of some urgency.

Issues for Discussion

As Mr Wherton, analyse the problem and be ready to present your recommendations, with reasons, to the Board of Aeropa.

Acknowledgement

We are grateful to Mr J. C. Hull, of Cranfield Management School, for help in the preparation of this case.

5 Quantock Plastics Ltd: A Further Machine
(Written as at 1970)

Introduction

Finar International Ltd is a large holding company based in London. It has several subsidiary companies, the majority of which are located in old Commonwealth countries and in Europe. Although originally registered as Finar Ltd, substantial domestic and international expansion precipitated both a change in title and, at the same time, a rapidly increasing diversification of interests. In the early days of operation its main interests lay in the manufacture of heavy and speciality chemicals, but the gradual overall expansion facilitated involvement in new areas of production. Among such acquisitions were a large paper company, several plastic convertors, and a number of small companies which were engaged in various areas of plastics applications. This particular case study examines a problem confronting one such subsidiary, namely Quantock Plastics Ltd.

By way of introduction it is useful to study the basic breakdown of the Plastics Division within the parent company. The Plastics Division comprised seven companies, of varying size and technical sophistication, but with an overall emphasis on the processing of bulk polymer to a variety of end products. The main processes involved were blow and injection moulding, thermo-forming, blowing and casting films, whilst, to a lesser extent, plastic adhesives were also represented. However, it should be noted that Finar International was not strongly involved in the manufacture of bulk polymer, nor was there any question of vertical integration.

Quantock Plastics was located in the West Country, and was the sole producer of plastics films within the Plastics Division of Finar International. Its two most important production processes were blowing and casting.

In terms of a simplified technical explanation, blow film is produced by melting a polymer such as polythene or nylon, and extruding it vertically through a thin, annular ring. This in turn is itself cooled by the blowing of compressed air through its centre. The result of this operation is a large, vertical, sausage-shaped balloon of rapidly cooling plastic, which is deflated over a series of rollers, and finally wound into a reel. This reel of doubled material is subsequently slit along one edge to produce a wide (120-inch), thin (approx 1/1,000-inch) film. Although this process is somewhat slow when compared to possible alternatives, it has the comparative dual advantages of being relatively inexpensive in terms of capital outlay for machinery, and the equipment itself is easy to run.

In the early 1960s Quantock Plastics had produced only blown film. Nevertheless this had not implied any lack of general interest in learning about relevant innovations, either in England or from abroad. During the latter part of 1965 a lengthy visit to North America had been made by a group of managers and research experts. For the most part, this visit had been inspection tours of numerous companies engaged in activities similar to those undertaken by Quantock. It had been during this visit that the managers had become particularly excited about the market possibilities for coextruded film, and it had been decided to initiate a thorough study of the situation in relation to the United Kingdom market.

The Coextrusion Process

The process of coextrusion is one by which two molten plastic films are united at the moment of extrusion. The comparative advantage of two-ply films is that the properties of the individual components can complement each other. That is, a film with good oxygen barrier properties could be married to one with high mechanical strength. This method has proved particularly useful in providing an economical method of utilizing high-cost plastic films, largely because a thin film of the expensive resin can be coextruded with a thick film of a cheaper 'carrier' film.

At the time of the North American visit there had been ample supplies of two-ply films, obtained by the process of lacquer lamination. This process consisted of 'glueing' together two films which had previously been produced on blow extrusion machines. However, this method of production had not been very popular, largely because of the high production costs incurred. The high costs had resulted mainly from the lengthy time period required in order to allow adequate drying time for the lacquer glue. Another contributory factor towards the high cost level had been that the type of film which could be laminated by the process had to be thick enough to withstand mechanical handling and the cheaper range of available films had not, in general, been very suitable.

At the time of the working visit, the main process for coextrusion in North America had been a patented blowing process. It was the first process which had employed a method of guaranteeing the adhesion of two films. This had been achieved by introducing ozone into the space between two annular rings on a blowing unit. The combination of gas with any of the common blowing plastics had virtually guaranteed a powerful bond.

During the period of the American visit there had been increasing industrial interest in the feasibility of alternative processes of manufacture. A number of US convertors had commissioned coextrusion casting machines with the express intention of overcoming the tight patent coverage on the blowing process.

Again to refer to the technical aspect of this process, the operation of casting film is carried out by melting a plastic resin and forcing it through a narrow slit in a steel barrel so as to form a curtain of molten plastic which falls onto an ice-water-cooled chill roller. The plastic cools, sets, and is then wound up into a reel. Coextrusion is obtained by using two chill rollers. The adhesion is promoted by the use of an arc discharge tube situated between the films, and whilst this is not as effective as the ozone system convertors, it was found in practice that, if the machines were carefully controlled when in use, and if the running conditions were meticulously observed, then the resulting standard of film was acceptable for most purposes.

Technical and Market Trials

Recognizing its own interest in the possibility of developing the use of the coextrusion film, Quantock Plastics initiated technical and marketing trials.

As far as the technical experts had been concerned, the outcome of the tests had been highly satisfactory. It appeared that the range of films which could be produced by blowing and casting was fairly similar, although a higher level of expertise was required in the case of the latter. The capital cost of a casting machine was higher, but it operated at higher speeds and it compared favourably with the blowing machine in terms of royalty payments. The process produced a film surface of very even thickness, and the general assessment of the finished product had been that it was likely to be more satisfactory than that offered by the alternative process. Research work had suggested that even thickness was of prime importance in the potential market areas. It had accordingly been decided to enter into a joint 'know-how' agreement with an American convertor, namely Albany Packaging Inc. This agreement meant that the joint resources of the two companies had been used to design and build a coextrusion casting machine, which was known as C1. This machine had been put into operation within one year from the initiation of negotiations with Albany Packaging. However, it had been found necessary to spend an additional six months on redesigning, adding refinements, and giving intensive operator training. C1 had been eventually passed to the production department towards the end of 1966.

In addition to the comprehensive technical research, Quantock had also implemented extensive market research work. Somewhat predictable results had been reached, and it was reaffirmed that much of the shift in market emphasis was closely related to changes in the internal structure of the company. In the early 1960s the company's principal interests had been in the sphere of the heavy end of the plastic film business. The main products had been heavy-duty coloured polythene films for agricultural, building, and industrial usage. Internal personnel changes had been reflected in a massive transfer of interest towards more sophisticated markets. For example, the appointment of a new commercial director (prior to his appointment he had been involved closely with speciality chemical marketing) was quickly followed by an extensive review of marketing policies or, to be more accurate, of the lack of such policies. As a result, Quantock Plastics had taken a deeper interest in the market for packaging films. This new emphasis had been allied to a necessary growth in the level of expertise regarding finer gauge films and the more esoteric plastics. The new customers had tended to be mainly traditional flexible packaging convertors, who laminated the films to paper or aluminium foil, printed them, and then sold them to pharmaceutical, detergent, toiletries, and confectionery manufacturers. In addition a few contracts had been obtained with end-use manufacturers, who printed the plain films that Quantock Plastics supplied. The level of success that had been achieved in these areas was probably a highly influential factor in the final decision to install coextrusion capacity, as had been the prospect of the continuing expansion of the market for packaged goods, and thus simultaneously for packaging films.

Installation of New Machines

In view of the overall positive reaction from both technical and market research studies, it had been decided to install a coextrusion casting machine. Indeed Quantock Plastics had been the first company in the United Kingdom to do so. Despite the existence of several blowing units which had used the patented American system, Quantock had been able to acquire a large share of the available market within a very short space of time. This had been achieved largely because of a small price advantage over the blown machines and a much more favourable selling price than laminated films. The revitalized commercial department had pioneered new uses, and hence new customers. Within two years the expanding market had necessitated the operation of three-shift capacity on C1.

Towards the end of 1968 John Chisholm had been appointed Managing Director of Quantock Plastics. This appointment had been concurrent with the establishment of a study group to assess whether or not the company should purchase a second coextrusion machine. The Review Group reported during the early part of 1969, and the result had been a foregone conclusion. Indeed the principal problem had been seen to be one of how to contain demand until the new machine could be installed. In March 1969 Finar International had authorized the capital requisition for C2, and the machine's installation had been scheduled for June or July of that year, with the anticipation that it would be fully operational during 1971. The Group also recommended that the position be reviewed midway through 1971 since market forecasts indicated that it might be necessary to acquire a third machine in 1972.

On 8 April 1970 Mr Chisholm was told by his immediate superior from the parent company that the opportunity of buying a coextrusion machine existed. As far as Finar International was concerned the selling price was considered low, and it was felt that such an acquisition would be advantageous for either Quantock Plastics or for one of the Australian subsidiaries. The machine was being put on the market by Purfleet Paper, who had been unable to operate the machine either economically or efficiently. The sale was deemed necessary to aid pressing cash flow problems and they hoped that the sale would raise £50,000. Purfleet had requested an early decision, specifying a date ten days hence, after which time the machine would be offered elsewhere.

John Kendall, who represented Finar International, suggested that Mr Chisholm appoint a Review Team delegated with the responsibility of evaluating the current situation.

A Review Team was subsequently nominated, headed by Mr Chisholm. He was assisted by six specialists from within the company:

Peter Sadler	Corporate Planner
Don Edwards	Production Director
Alan Ryan	Chief Accountant
Vernon Ould	Market Analyst
Paul Artis	Engineering Manager
Ted Osborne	Coextrusion Department Manager

Don Edwards's immediate reaction was that it would be impossible to complete the required study within the time horizon specified. He had himself been a member of the C2 study group, and, despite intensive work on the part of that group, the final report had taken three months of trials and evaluation before it was ready for presentation. In any case, he thought it essential to run trials on the machine before he would be prepared to offer any opinion. He saw this as a valid excuse for requesting the postponement of the decision date, and anticipated that, at a minimum, two weeks would be required to complete any preliminary assessment. Purfleet Paper were contacted, and they agreed to arrange for trials to be run on Monday, 20 April. At the same time they volunteered to answer any queries that Quantock might have in relation to the machine and its operation, and Mr Osborne was given the opportunity to make free contact with the Technical Manager at Purfleet.

The Review Study

The major part of the Review Team's study consisted of updating the C2 evaluation. It was felt that the amount of new data required was minimal, although there were certain key issues which had to be assessed. In particular it was felt prudent to look closely at the following areas:

(i) The last market forecast had been presented in 1969. How reliable was the information that had been received since that date, how up-to-date was it, and had any new trends emerged?

(ii) Was the Purfleet machine capable of handling the same range of films as was possible when using the C1 and C2 models? It was generally felt that the machine was able to do so, but this opinion had to be confirmed.

(iii) How would the price/volume relationship change? What were the likely changes in the price of bulk polymer? Would prices soften as capacity caught up with demand?

(iv) What level of manning was required? What were the likely increases in wage rates, and how rapid were such escalations likely to be?

(v) General queries regarding the storage of the machine, associated stocks of raw materials and finished products. Where could these items be housed; would it be necessary to convert the existing resin store and build a new warehouse elsewhere on the factory site? What expenditure would be likely to be entailed?

(vi) What were the anticipated costs of reinstallation?

It was decided that the proposal should be evaluated on a net present value basis, giving 'most likely', 'optimistic', and 'pessimistic' forecasts.

The results of the investigations were discussed at a meeting held a week later, and the data prepared by Mr Sadler are shown in Appendix 1.

In calculating the NPVs, it was necessary to make a number of basic assumptions. These included:

(i) The machine would not be commissioned until mid-1971. This decision was reached in view of the shortage of engineering personnel and because the C2 machine would not be commissioned until Christmas.

(ii) Previous market forecasts had proved to be fairly reliable, and it was felt that these were acceptable in their present form. (See Appendix 2.) It was therefore agreed to use the estimate of 25-per-cent average market share in future calculations and analyses.

(iii) Even allowing for pessimistic assumptions, demand was forecast to grow at 6 per cent per annum.

(iv) The analysis shows only the incremental sales, derived directly from the use of the Purfleet machine.

(v) Estimates of the breakdown of capital costs as shown in Appendix 3.

Ancillary equipment would be needed for slitting and rewinding whenever new extruding capacity was installed. At a minimum, it would be essential to have one slitter and two rewinders. In terms of manpower, it was considered necessary to assume that three-shift working would be needed to operate the machines. However, it was felt that only under the pessimistic assumptions would it be necessary to build the new resin store.

It was found too difficult and too time-consuming to produce the three different figures (most likely, optimistic, and pessimistic) for any of the unknowns other than market forecasts. It was also difficult to reach any level of consensus on what was meant by these three outcomes. However, it was eventually agreed that the chance of the optimistic forecast occurring was 0·2, that of the most likely forecast occurring was 0·45, and that of the most pessimistic occurring was 0·35.

The question of probabilities aroused some controversy. The three points chosen were simply arbitrary points from a continuous distribution. It was suggested that it might have been more useful to define the probabilities first (say, $\frac{1}{4}$, $\frac{1}{2}$, and $\frac{1}{4}$, or $\frac{1}{3}$, $\frac{1}{3}$ and $\frac{1}{3}$) and then adjust the market forecasts accordingly.

Mr Sadler agreed to look at the problem in view of these suggestions.

Some other assumptions made were:

(i) Tax rate 40 per cent.
(ii) Investment grant was low as the machine was second-hand.
(iii) Working capital was 50 per cent of value-added.
(iv) Scrap value would be zero after ten years.
(v) 80 per cent of working capital would be recoverable.
(vi) 17-per-cent discount rate was used (required by the group for new capacity projects).

Although the DCF, *discounted cash flow*, calculations showed that the proposal would be profitable under all except pessimistic assumptions, it was felt that it would be sensible to consider other possibilities.

Further Alternatives

After further discussions it was decided to consider three other alternatives:

(i) To use the basic features of C2 in designing a new machine to be called C3. The principal disadvantage of such a strategy would be one of time wastage.
(ii) Purchase the Purfleet machine, but cannibalize it with parts of the C1 machine and produce a machine of the same capacity as the C2.
(iii) Use the basic assumption of Proposal (ii) above, but cannibalize the Purfleet and C1 machines to produce a machine capable of triple extrusion. The triple-extrusion model was becoming increasingly popular in the American market, and it was felt that such a model might be a viable proposition for use in the domestic market. The main disadvantage of this strategy would be that extensive design work would be essential.

At this stage in the discussion there remained one week in which the Review Team could reach a final decision as to the most favourable strategy to adopt. This week was used to perform essential basic trials. These proved satisfactory, and it was concluded that Purfleet had suffered operational problems largely as a result of their own lack of experience with extruding.

Appendices 4 and 5 show the DCF calculations on the first two of these new proposals. It was found that the third one was a non-starter, as the machine could only have been operated at half normal speed, which meant that it was not profitable, even under optimistic assumptions.

The following points were noted about the new proposals. The C3 machine was expected to cost £100,000 more than the C2 machine. This estimate included allowances for increased prices, modifications, and additions, and the inclusion of the new resin store. The £120,000 for modifications of the C1 included one extra slitting machine for operation on two shifts. After consultation with manufacturers it was discovered that, by using the Purfleet machine for the cannibalization, the cost would be only 60 per cent of the likely expenditure, should the work be started from scratch.

Even given this information, there was still much disagreement about which strategy should be adopted. Putting the Purfleet machine into operation would have the highest return for the 'most likely' and 'optimistic' cases, but would have a negative NPV for the 'pessimistic' case. On the other hand, the cannibalization alternative would have a positive NPV for all outcomes.

Since both these alternatives would indicate that the Purfleet machine should be purchased, Mr Edwards pointed out that it would be sensible to put forward an offer. The decision as to what should be done with the machine could be delayed until Christmas by which time there would be far more information readily available.

However, Mr Sadler had not reached the same conclusion and he was not so ready to reject the C3 alternative as out of hand. He believed that the lower NPV values of the C3 proposal in contrast to those of the Purfleet machines were mainly because it could not have been installed until mid-1972. This meant that there were two extra years before an irreversible decision had to be made. Thus, initial design studies could be undertaken on this alternative at a very low cost and therefore they could, in effect, collect some information about C3 before committing themselves to a final decision.

Mr Sadler argued that two years' sales data would change the likelihoods of the various forecasts being correct. For example, two years 'high' sales would increase the probability of the 'optimistic' outcome occurring. He asked Mr Ould, the market analyst, to quantify this. Mr Ould agreed that, at the present time, the probabilities of the optimistic, most likely, and pessimistic forecasts being correct were 0·2, 0·45, and 0·35 respectively. Next, Mr Sadler asked him to assume that the 1971 sales data were also high. Mr Ould thought that the probabilities of optimistic, most likely, and pessimistic outcomes were 0·9, 0·1 and 0·0 respectively. This procedure was followed for all permutations of sales data, and the results are shown in Appendix 6.

Mr Edwards was somewhat overawed by the range of possible alternatives, and he therefore asked Mr Sadler if he could, given the time constraint facing the company, see a systematic approach which could be adopted in an attempt to resolve the problem.

Appendix 1 Information on the Purchase of Coextrusion Machine from Purfleet Paper on Packaging

(1) Optimistic

	1971	1972	1973	1974	1975	1976	1977	1978	1979
Additional Sales*	800	2,100	2,100	2,100	2,100	2,100	2,100	2,100	2,100
Additional Value added	168	432	424	416	407	399	390	382	374
Additional Overhead	-110	-119	-130	-141	-152	-164	-177	-191	-206
Additional Tax	-17	-119	-112	-104	-96	-88	-80	-71	-121
Additional Fixed capital	-170								
Additional Grant		+20							
Additional Working capital	-84	-132	4	4	4	4	4	4	150
Additional Cash flow	-213	82	186	175	164	152	139	125	197

Net Present Value = 445

(2) Most Likely

	1971	1972	1973	1974	1975	1976	1977	1978	1979
Additional Sales	700	1,200	1,580	1,870	2,100	2,100	2,100	2,100	2,100
Additional Value added	147	247	319	370	407	399	390	382	374
Additional Overhead	-110	-119	-130	-141	-152	-164	-177	-191	-206
Additional Tax	-9	-45	-70	-86	-96	-88	-79	-70	-121
Additional Fixed capital	-170								
Additional Grants		+20							
Additional Working capital	-73	-50	-36	-25	-18	+4	+4	+4	+150
Additional Cash flow	-215	53	83	118	141	151	138	125	197

Net Present Value = 189

* Sales in tons; other values in £000.

Appendix 1 (*contd*)

(3) Pessimistic

Additional Sales	130	580	950	1,080	1,360	1,580	1,810	2,010	2,100
Additional Value added	27	120	192	214	264	300	336	366	374
Additional Overhead	−110	−119	−130	−141	−152	−164	−177	−191	−206
Additional Tax	41	5	−17	−21	−37	−46	−56	−62	−119
Additional Fixed capital	−230								
Additional Grants		30							
Additional Working capital	−13	−47	−36	−11	−25	−18	−18	−15	150
Additional Cash flow	−285	−11	9	41	50	72	85	98	199

Net Present Value = 60

Appendix 2 Market Forecasts for Coextruded Plastic Films
1970–79 (tons)

	1967	1968	1969	1970	1971	1972	1973	1974	1975	1976	1977	1978	1979
Total market : Actual	4,800	9,200	15,000										
Quantock sales : Actual	1,200	1,800	1,800										
Optimistic													
Total market : Forecast				24,300	28,400	31,400	33,000	34,300	35,000	35,000	35,000	35,000	35,000
Quantock : Forecast				6,030	7,100	7,850	8,260	8,590	8,750	8,750	8,750	8,750	8,750
Quantock : Capacity				3,100	6,100	7,400	7,400	7,400	7,400	7,400	7,400	7,400	7,400
Most likely													
Total market : Forecast				21,000	24,100	26,200	27,500	28,700	29,800	30,500	31,000	32,000	32,500
Quantock : Forecast				5,250	6,000	6,500	6,880	7,170	7,450	7,630	7,760	8,000	8,130
Quantock : Capacity				3,100	6,100	7,400	7,400	7,400	7,400	7,400	7,400	7,400	7,400
Pessimistic													
Total market : Forecast				19,300	21,700	23,500	25,000	25,500	26,600	27,500	28,400	29,200	30,000
Quantock : Forecast				4,830	5,430	5,880	6,250	6,380	6,660	6,880	7,110	7,310	7,500
Quantock : Capacity				3,100	6,100	7,400	7,400	7,400	7,400	7,400	7,400	7,400	7,400

Appendix 3 Capital Outlay on Purfleet Project

	£
Purchase price	50,000
Uplift, transport, reinstallation	25,000
Essential modifications and additions	25,000
Slitting machine	20,000
Two rewinding machines	35,000
Additional resin silo	10,000
Contingency	5,000
	170,000
Conversion of resin store to work in progress	15,000
New resin store	45,000
	60,000

Appendix 4 Purchase of a New Coextrusion Machine C3

(1) Optimistic

	1971	1972	1973	1974	1975	1976	1977	1978	1979
Additional Sales*		1,200	2,960	3,290	3,450	3,450	3,450	3,450	3,450
Additional Value added		247	598	652	670	655	643	628	614
Additional Overhead		−119	−130	−141	−152	−164	−177	−191	−206
Additional Tax		−35	−171	−188	−191	−180	−170	−159	−203
Additional Fixed capital		−500							
Additional Grants			100						
Additional Working capital		−123	−175	−27	−9	7	12	15	240
Additional Cash flow		−530	222	296	318	318	308	293	345

Net Present Value = 384

(2) Most Likely

	1971	1972	1973	1974	1975	1976	1977	1978	1979
Additional Sales		1,200	1,580	1,870	2,150	2,330	2,460	2,700	2,830
Additional Value added		247	319	370	417	443	458	492	504
Additional Overhead		−119	−130	−141	−152	−164	−177	−191	−206
Additional Tax		−35	−60	−76	−90	−96	−97	−104	−274
Additional Fixed capital		−500							
Additional Grants			100						
Additional Working capital		−123	−36	−25	−24	−13	−7	−17	200
Additional Cash flow		−530	193	128	151	170	177	180	430

Net Present Value = 131

* Sales in tons; other values in £000.

Appendix 4 (contd)

(3) Pessimistic

Additional Sales	580	950	1,080	1,360	1,580	1,810	2,010	2,200
Additional Value added	119	192	214	264	300	337	366	392
Additional Overhead	−119	−130	−141	−152	−164	−177	−191	−206
Additional Tax	16	−9	−13	−29	−39	−48	−54	−122
Additional Fixed capital	−500							
Additional Grants		100						
Additional Working capital	−59	−36	−11	−25	−18	−18	−15	160
Additional Cash flow	−425	118	49	58	79	94	106	224

Net Present Value = −33

Appendix 5 Modification of Existing C1 to C2 Standards

(1) Optimistic

	1971	1972	1973	1974	1975	1976	1977	1978	1979
Additional Sales*	−500	1,100	1,100	1,100	1,100	1,100	1,100	1,100	1,100
Additional Value added	−105	227	222	218	213	209	205	200	196
Additional Overhead	−5	−10	−11	−12	−13	−14	−15	−17	−19
Additional Tax	47	−84	−81	−79	−77	−75	−73	−70	−100
Additional Fixed capital	−120								
Additional Grants		10							
Additional Working capital	−52	−61	2	2	2	2	2	2	80
Additional Cash flow	−235	82	132	129	125	122	119	115	147

Net Present Value = 192

(2) Most Likely

	1971	1972	1973	1974	1975	1976	1977	1978	1979
Additional Sales	−500	1,100	1,100	1,100	1,100	1,100	1,100	1,100	1,100
Additional Value added	−105	227	222	218	213	209	205	200	196
Additional Overhead	−5	−10	−11	−12	−13	−14	−15	−17	−19
Additional Tax	47	−84	−81	−79	−77	−75	−73	−70	−100
Additional Fixed capital	−120								
Additional Grants		10							
Additional Working capital	−52	−61	2	2	2	2	2	2	80
Additional Cash flow	−235	82	132	129	125	122	119	115	147

Net Present Value = 192

* Sales in tons; other values in £000.

Appendix 5 (contd)

(3) Pessimistic

Additional Sales	-500	580	950	1,080	1,100	1,100	1,100	1,100	1,100
Additional Value added	-105	119	192	214	213	209	205	200	196
Additional Overhead	-5	-10	-11	-12	-13	-14	-15	-17	-19
Additional Tax	47	-40	-69	-79	-77	-75	-13	-70	-100
Additional Fixed capital	-120								
Additional Grants	-52	-7	-36	-11	2	2	2	2	80
Additional Working capital	10								
Additional Cash flow	-235	72	76	112	123	122	119	115	147

Net Present Value = 137

Appendix 6 Probability of Various Forecasts in Light of Additional Information

Category	Probability of forecast now	Probability if 1970 sales data is:		Probability if additionally 1971 sales data is:	
Optimistic	0·2	High	0·6	High	0·9
				Medium	0·7
				Low	0·5
		Medium	0·2	High	0·4
				Medium	0·05
				Low	0·0
		Low	0·1	High	0·3
				Medium	0·0
				Low	0·0
Most Likely	0·45	High	0·3	High	0·1
				Medium	0·2
				Low	0·3
		Medium	0·6	High	0·5
				Medium	0·9
				Low	0·7
		Low	0·1	High	0·4
				Medium	0·2
				Low	0·0
Pessimistic	0·35	High	0·1	High	0·0
				Medium	0·1
				Low	0·2
		Medium	0·2	High	0·1
				Medium	0·05
				Low	0·3
		Low	0·8	High	0·3
				Medium	0·8
				Low	1·0

6 Maybury Company: New Product Launch
(Written as at 1971)

Company Background

British Confectionery Ltd has grown from a two-man partnership established in 1910 to a limited company which, with its subsidiaries, now operates all over the world. The largest company in the group is Maybury, which contributes about a third of the group's turnover of £65 million. It manufactures toffee, fudge, peppermints, boiled sweets, and butterscotch, but its main business still relies on the production of toffee which was the original product of the firm.

Because of the growth, almost to saturation point, of the market for these lines, aggressive policies for the establishment of individually branded and distinctive lines have become essential. Increasingly, brand names have come to be used to identify unique products. They are associated with a single, clearly differentiated product and, since they are not descriptive names, advertising is of paramount importance to establish them in the public mind. In addition to the high degree of competition within the confectionery industry, the industry has itself to compete with producers of many other related commodities such as ice-cream, cigarettes, alcohol, and soft drinks, which are the subjects of intensive promotional campaigns. These developments in branding and advertising have increased the monetary risks of establishing a new brand, since the process may take about three years and necessitates an investment in advertising over this period that may be several times as great as the investment in the plant required to manufacture the new line.

Part A
The New Product Decision I

The Maybury Board of Directors have agreed in principle to the launching of a new line and given the Marketing Group their

78

terms of reference for an investigation into the possible alternatives and their economic implications.

A meeting of the Marketing Group was convened with the intention of obtaining an initial appraisal of the potential of the new line using the information available. Because of the extent of product development and testing within the firm, it had developed its own field force to undertake consumer surveys, and the Marketing Director, Mr Dorland, intended to use these preliminary studies for a first analysis of the new product's performance.

Because of the cost of these consumer studies, Mr Dorland requested information relating to just three possible market share levels: 10 per cent, the desired target penetration which was constrained by the fierce competition; 6 per cent, a pessimistic assessment of the marketing objective; and 2 per cent which represented 'failure' of the campaign. He felt these three discrete levels would indicate how the product was likely to perform and were appropriate for a first appraisal. He intended ultimately to assess a distribution describing the whole continuum of possible market shares and to incorporate it into the analysis as a more realistic model at a later stage.

Maybury proposed to launch the new product with a national television campaign; an option only open to them owing to their size, since the cost of this advertising medium was high. The use of television raised new problems for the Marketing Group. It was likely to have a twofold effect on the introduction of the new line: firstly, by inducing the retailers to stock large quantities of the new line if they knew that it was to be promoted strongly on television and, secondly, by producing an initially high level of consumption which would not reflect repeat purchase behaviour, because successful television advertising depends on novelty. While the product was new, and before its novelty was replaced by a competing novelty, its sales were likely to be high – much higher in fact than the levels at which it was expected to sell steadily. In order to minimize the drop factor effect and obviate the use of production capacity which would be substantially in excess of the ultimate settle-down requirement, Maybury were considering a series of time-staggered regional introductions. Dorland suggested that they confine their considerations to this settle-down figure and volunteered that in his opinion the probability of the line achieving a 10-per-cent share of the market was 0·7 and for the other share levels of 6 per cent and 2 per cent was 0·1 and 0·2 respectively.

The Chairman of the Board of Maybury, Mr Gorlings, was also responsible for the research activities of the firm, so that it was in this capacity that he was present at the meeting of the Marketing Group. The research was carried out in laboratories which were sited next to the company's main factory. This was company policy: 'ivory tower' research was not encouraged; research was initiated by a request from within the company and subsequent investigation was based on clearly defined objectives. Gorlings made the point that, since the development costs for the new line had already been paid, they should not influence the decision as to whether to launch or not, so that in effect the cost of scrubbing the launch could be considered as zero.

Gorlings also believed that Dorland's probability assessments were somewhat optimistic; the chairman had been in the business a long time and had witnessed many new lines whose sales had settled down at too low a level to carry the large annual outlay of a full advertising campaign. He realized that none of the previously launched lines had achieved the sales figures of the first product since the war; but Gorlings was prepared to accept the figures and felt the rest of the group could do the same.

The Director for Home Sales, Mr Clive, concurred with the assessments and suggested that the corresponding profit contribution from the settle-down sales figures would be of the order of £1 million and £200,000 for the 10-per-cent and 6-per-cent market share levels respectively. He felt that, if the new line secured only a 2-per-cent share, then the launching would lose the company £600,000 as a result. Dorland felt they now had enough information to do an initial analysis of the situation which would incorporate his considered opinion with the objective data of the monetary outcomes from the 'expert', Mr Clive. (It is suggested that readers might wish to pause at this point and make their own evaluation of the situation facing Maybury and to draw the appropriate decision tree before reading on. The appropriate decision tree is shown in Exhibit 1.)

Part B
New Information I

The Maybury Company had used the services of Arrow Market Research Bureau in the past and had asked them to submit a research proposal for a test marketing of the new line. The Marketing Group decided to meet again to discuss whether it was worthwhile collecting extra market research information to throw further light upon the probability assessments of the unknown variable, market share, before taking the final decision. They agreed to let Dorland and Kitteridge submit an analysis to the Group for further discussion.

Kitteridge and Dorland secured a quiet office for an afternoon to try to determine the benefits of the research proposal. The objective of the analysis at this point was to ascertain *now* whether it would be economically worthwhile for Maybury to purchase additional information by quantifying the likely benefits of such information. To help set limits on the value of the research data, they considered the expected value of the strategy that yielded the largest payoff for each uncertain outcome; conceptually they were obtaining the optimal act under conditions of 'perfect information'. Such perfect information would enable them, for each outcome, to choose the best decision. Thus, for the higher (10-percent) and medium (6-per-cent) market shares, the optimal act would be to launch the product with the corresponding payoffs of £1 million and £200,000 respectively. However, should the lower (2-per-cent) market share be realized, the better strategy would be to scrap the product, incurring zero payoff. Hence the expected value of the strategy, adopted under conditions of perfect information, was the product of the maximal payoff multiplied by the assessed probability of occurrence of each market share, summed for the three possible market shares, which in this case means $0.7 \times £1,000,000 + 0.1 \times £200,000 - 0.2 \times £0$ or £720,000. The difference between this value and the maximum expected monetary value based on the initial assessments in the prior analysis provided Kitteridge and Dorland with an upper limit for the worth of additional information called the Expected Value of Perfect Information (EVPI), which they calculated to be £120,000. Hence, in the extreme case, if any market research bureau were to submit a proposal that cost £120,000 or more, Maybury should reject it out of hand since no bureau would presume that its information could be perfect.

However, the figure that Arrow had quoted for their market research proposal was £10,000. In addition to details of the agreed research design Arrow's proposal contained assessments of the reliability of their test market indications. For example, it showed that the results would indicate a high market share (Z_1) with a reliability of 60 per cent. That is to say, if the final settle-down market share for the new line was 10 per cent, then there was a 60-per-cent chance that it would achieve a high market share indication in the tested area. The reliability assessments are set out in full in Table 6.1. Note that the probabilities in each row of the table sum to 1. It is a coincidence that the columns sum similarly.

Table 6.1 Arrow's Judgement of the Reliability of their Test Market Indications

Sales level	Test market indication		
	Z_1 (high)	Z_2 (medium)	Z_3 (low)
10%: p_1	0·6	0·3	0·1
6%: p_2	0·3	0·6	0·1
2%: p_3	0·1	0·1	0·8

Z_1 = high market share indicated by testing
Z_2 = medium market share indicated by testing
Z_3 = low market share indicated by testing

Kitteridge and Dorland discussed at length the incorporation of the new information that would arise from the proposed market research and whether Maybury should hire the services of the external bureau, Arrow. Kitteridge explained that the figures in Table 6.1 were conditional probabilities, that is, they are of the form:

e.g. $P(Z_3/P_1) =$ Probability that test result indicates 'low' when the product's eventual share is 10 per cent.

Thus they are the likelihoods of each test result. Kitteridge then formulated Table 6.2 where the final column contains the revised probabilities for the occurrence of the three market levels for each test market indication. These revised or posterior probabilities are obtained by weighting Dorland's initial probability assessments with the likelihoods given in Table 6.1 and 'normalizing' them. Hence the revised probability of achieving a market share of 10 per cent given a high test market indication (the first entry in column 5 of Table 6.2) will be the likelihood of achieving a high test indication given a prevailing 10-per-cent market (0·6 from Table 6.1) weighted by Dorland's opinion of the probability that a 10-per-cent market will prevail (0·7) and divided by the total probability of achieving a high indication (by calculation, 0·47).

Table 6.2 Revised Probabilities Incorporating Market Research Information

(1)	(2)	(3)	(4)	(5)
Test outcome	prior probability of outcome, i.e. Dorland's initial assessments	Likelihood of test outcome (from Table 6.1)	Col. (2) × Col. (3)	Revised or posterior probability of outcome
Z_1: Sample result indicates high market share	p_1: market share 10%: 0·7 p_2: market share 6%: 0·1 p_3: market share 2%: 0·2	0·6 0·3 0·1 $P(Z_1) = 0·47$	0·42 0·03 0·02	0·90 0·06 0·04
Z_2: Sample result indicates medium market share	p_1: 0·7 p_2: 0·1 p_3: 0·2	0·3 0·6 0·1 $P(Z_2) = 0·29$	0·21 0·06 0·02	0·72 0·21 0·07
Z_3: Sample result indicates low market share	p_1: 0·7 p_2: 0·1 p_3: 0·2	0·1 0·1 0·8 $P(Z_3) = 0·24$	0·07 0·01 0·16	0·29 0·04 0·67

At the end of the afternoon Dorland and Kitteridge felt they now had enough information to submit a revised analysis incorporating these probabilities for the next meeting of the Marketing Group. (Readers may wish to pause again at this point to make their own evaluation of the new situation in the form of a decision tree. The appropriate decision tree is shown in Exhibits 2 and 3.)

Part C
A Further Model

Having completed their analysis and reported to the Marketing Group, Dorland and Kitteridge readdressed themselves to the market share level assessments and the ensuing analyses based upon them. For their initial analyses they had accepted the approximation of confining their attention to three discrete levels rather than a density distribution over the complete range of possible market shares. They now reviewed the problem, replacing the event fork consisting of just three levels by a multiple event fork, that is a continuous distribution. Kitteridge explained that the distribution describing Dorland's judgement concerning the new product's likely performance could be retrieved from his replies to three questions. Kitteridge proposed to encode Dorland's opinion by a particular curve from a comprehensive set of probability density functions called the 'Beta' family. From Dorland's replies to the questions Kitteridge could solve a set of equations for the particular parameters that would describe Dorland's opinion. Kitteridge volunteered to undertake the 'mathematics' of the solution. Once the particular curve had been ascertained, Kitteridge suggested that they review the model for the consideration of Arrow's proposal for additional market research. He maintained that the analysis should consist of the following:

The curve representing Dorland's prior opinion concerning the new product's future market shares. (See Part D below.)

A curve representing Arrow's likely market research results.

The combination of the two curves to derive a final curve portraying Dorland's revised opinion based on an expected value of the proposed market research. (See Part E below.)

They proceeded along these lines.

Part D
The New Product Decision II

Dorland was able to summarize his knowledge relating to the market share p, in the form of a probability density function, by answering the following questions:

(a) If you had to make a single 'best' assessment; what do you think the product's most likely market share will be?

(b) What do you feel the chances are that the market share will be less than or equal to 10 per cent?

Dorland asked Kitteridge to remind him of the meaning of 'most likely', and, after some discussion, decided that if he had to put his money on one single value he would choose 11 per cent. He was more confident in replying to the second question: he assessed the probability to be 0·25 that the market share would be less than 10 per cent. The two parameters used to describe the curve could be retrieved from his replies, but, as a consistency check to ensure that the particular Beta curve was truly representative of his feelings, Kitteridge asked one more question:

(c) What is the realistic upper bound to the possible share that the product could attain?

Dorland laughed, and replied that there was no possibility of the product obtaining more than half of the market.

Kitteridge's analysis to retrieve the particular Beta curve from Dorland's replies then proceeded as follows:

The Beta family of distributions has the general form:

(1) $f(p) = \dfrac{(n'-1)!}{(r'-1)! \, (n'-r'-1)! \, p^{r'-1} \, (1-p)^{\,n'-r'-1}}$

for $0 \leqslant p \leqslant 1$

where p is the unknown market share expressed as a decimal figure between 0 and 1.

From Dorland's reply to the first question the mode or most likely market share value was 11 per cent or 0·11. The two unknowns in equation (1) are n' and r'; these are the *parameters* of the distribution and once their values have been assessed the only unknown in the equation will be p, the market share. From general distribution theory the mode for distribution (1) is given by $\dfrac{r'-1}{n'-2}$, so that from Dorland's first reply the first equation to solve for n' and r' is as follows:

$$0·11 = \frac{r'-1}{n'-2}$$

and since 0·11 is approximately $\frac{1}{9}$ this becomes equivalently

$$\frac{r'-1}{n'-2} = \frac{1}{9}$$

which by simple rearrangement becomes

$$n' = 9r'-7 \tag{A}$$

The second question relates to the 0·25 fractile of Dorland's subjective distribution, that is to say he felt there was a probability of 0·25 that the value of p would be less than 10 per cent or 0·1. In mathematical notation

$$P(p \leqslant 0·1) = 0·25$$

Kitteridge referred to the relevant page from a comprehensive set of beta fractile tables. (See Appendix 3.) These tables give values of fractiles for Beta distributions described by different values of n and r. The particular values of n' and r' that will identify Dorland's prior distribution are determined by equation (A). Hence he searched the tables for a combination of n and r values whose 0·25 fractile is 0·1 and whose values satisfy equation (A). For example, when $r' = 1$ and $n' = 2$, equation (A) is satisfied, but this combination has a value of 0·2500 for the 0·25 fractile and hence was rejected. When $r' = 2$ and $n' = 11$, equation (A) is satisfied and the value of its 0·25 fractile is 0·0964 which is approximately 0·1 so this combination satisfies the criterion collected in the first two questions. The last question which served to ensure consistency revealed that in Dorland's opinion there was no possibility of the new product obtaining more than half of the market, which equivalently means that his distribution should be contained in the range of p: 0 to 50 per cent or 0 to 0·50. For $r' = 2$, $n' = 11$ from the table

$$P(p \leqslant 0·5) = 0·99$$

that is to say there is a probability of 0·99 (nearly 1) that p will be in the range 0 to 0·5. Hence the values of the parameters of Dorland's distribution were $r' = 2$ and $n' = 11$. Substitution of these values in equation (1) reduces the distribution to:

$$f(p) = 90p(1-p)^8$$

Kitteridge drew the curve illustrated in Appendix 1 derived from the data shown in Exhibit 4. He explained that Dorland's opinion was equivalent to taking a small sample of 11 consumers and finding that 2 of them purchased the new line. The size of the 'equivalent' sample indicated Dorland's confidence in the assessment and in this sense his prior judgement was said to be relatively vague. Dorland accepted this, stating that the 'concentration' of his judgement at the lower end of the market share range around 11 per cent adequately reflected his belief. The statistic summarizing the distribution was the expected market share, which in this case was 18 per cent given in general by r/n.

Part E
New Information II

Dorland and Kitteridge went on to reconsider the model adopted for describing Arrow's reliability. Kitteridge hypothesized that, since the survey was to be based on several samples, randomly drawn from within population groups whose purchasing behaviour was expected to be similar, the sampling design satisfied the criteria for describing the process by a Binomial probability distribution. Arrow had been able to describe their likely performance in the discretized share approximations by supplying conditional probabilities of the form $P(Z/p)$, that is to say their reliability *given* a market share p.

If the samples to be taken by Arrow satisfied the Binomial sampling criterion, consideration of the reliability of the test market was no longer relevant. The successful results, that is to say the number of consumers (r) who purchase the new product, will depend on the true population of people who will in the event purchase, and also on the size of the samples drawn from that population. Dorland's opinion concerning the true population of purchasers had been assessed, and the size of sample had been set at 100. Kitteridge analytically derived the unconditional distribution of r which was a Beta – Binomial function whose parameters were n (the sample size, 100 in this case), r' and n' (the parameters describing Dorland's prior opinion, which were 2 and 11 respectively). He used the expected value of this distribution as an estimate of the results yet to be obtained, which indicated that 18 of the 100 sampled consumers would purchase.

Kitteridge reviewed the discrete case and explained that the revised or posterior probabilities that he had calculated in Table 2 could now be replaced by a revised probability distribution. This posterior distribution was analogously obtained by weighting the prior distribution with the likelihood distribution summarized by its expected value. The distribution came from the same family as the prior distribution, namely the Beta family, and its parameters were r'' and n'' which depended on the parameters of the prior distribution (r', n') and the likelihood distribution r, as follows:

(a) $r'' = r' + r$
where r' is 2, and an appropriate estimate of r is 18 giving $r'' = 20$

(b) $n'' = n' + n$
where n' is 11 and n is 100, the size of the sample giving $n'' = 111$

Kitteridge now drew the posterior distribution (see Appendix 2 and the data derivation in Exhibit 2) and explained that, because Dorland's prior opinions were equivalent to a small sample of 11, the posterior distribution had been greatly influenced by the sampling data which used a sample of 100. In addition, the distribution was more symmetrical and peaked at 18 per cent, which was also the mean value of the distribution, in comparison to the corresponding values of 11 per cent and 18 per cent that were derived from Dorland's prior judgements.

The distribution reflected the belief concerning the likelihood of obtaining different market levels based on a summary statistic for r, the successful results. Hence, *before* the results are received, the likely change in information can be observed; for example, as one would expect, more information reduced the uncertainty concerning the market share as reflected by the spread of the distributions. (The parameter n'' of 111 indicating greater confidence than n' of the prior distribution.) After completion of the test market, if the results are on average very different from the calculated 18, the posterior distribution will be increasingly influenced by the sample results rather than the prior distribution. This follows, since incorporation of continued sampling from the true population will produce a posterior distribution which more closely describes the true situation than the prior distribution did. Moreover, if Dorland's judgement had been very much in error, more sampling would be required to reach a true description than if he had been very correct in his original assessments.

The distributions I and II were presented to the Marketing Group. Kitteridge reported that the second analysis confirmed their initial calculation although 'the numbers were different'. (Readers may wish to work through this latter analysis for themselves, see Exhibit 6.) Kitteridge felt that, in addition to the greater insight achieved by assessing the whole continuum of market shares, the more realistic model highlighted the importance of the *size* of samples to be commissioned from Arrow, which for these reports had been set at 100.

Issues for Discussion

(1) The case outlines an approach for calculating an upper limit to a market research budget. Contrast this approach with any other approaches of which you are aware.

(2) With hindsight, would you describe Dorland's initial assessment of the three market share levels in Part B as arbitrary?

(3) Discuss the relevance of the size of the sample commissioned from Arrow in Part E.

References

Further discussion of the methods used in this analysis are contained in:

PRATT, J. W., RAIFFA, H., and SCHLAIFER, R., *Introduction to Statistical Decision Theory*, McGraw-Hill, 1965, Chapter 11.

RAIFFA, H., and SCHLAIFER, R., *Applied Statistical Decision Theory*, Harvard University, 1961, Chapter 9.

Appendix 1 The Prior Distribution Describing Dorland's Judgements Concerning the Market Share

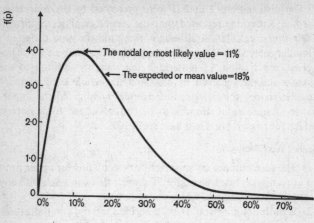

Appendix 2 The Posterior Distribution of Market Share Based on the Expected Value of Positive Results r from the Samples of 100, and Dorland's Prior Distribution in Appendix 1

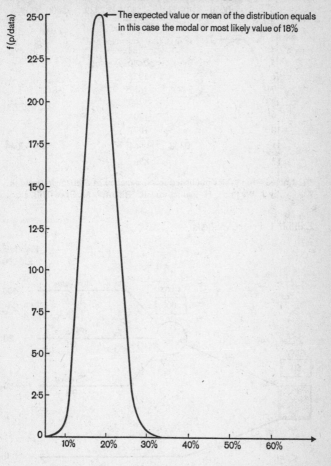

The expected value or mean of the distribution equals in this case the modal or most likely value of 18%

Appendix 3 Fractiles of the Beta Distribution*

	n	·01	·05	·25	·5	·75	·99
r = 1	2	·0100	·0500	·2500	·5000	·7500	·9900
	3	·0050	·0253	·1340	·2929	·5000	·9
	4			·0914			
r = 2	4			·3264			
	5			·2430			
	6			·1938			
	7			·1612			
	8			·1380			
	9			·1206			
	10			·1072			
	11		·0368	·0964			·5044
	12			·876			

* Extracted from tables published in *Introduction to Statistical Decision Theory*, by J. W. Pratt, H. Raiffa, and R. Schlaifer, McGraw-Hill, 1965.

Exhibit 1 Prior Analysis

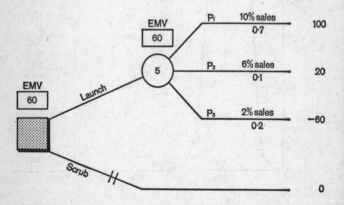

Exhibit 2 Decision Tree Analysis for Test Market

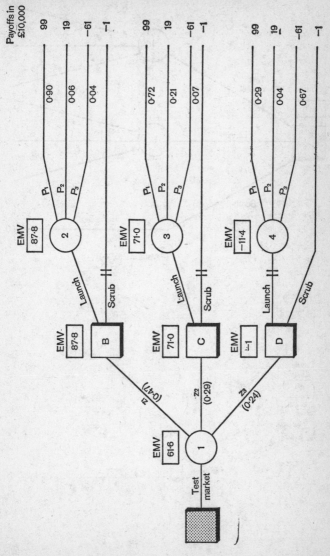

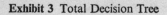

Exhibit 3 Total Decision Tree

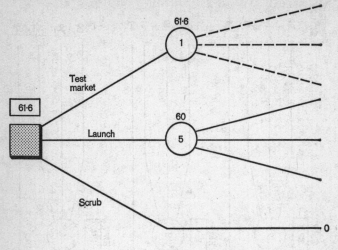

(Payoffs in £10,000)

94

Exhibit 4 The Prior Distribution

$$f(p) = 90p(1-p)^8$$

The program below computed a series of values for the distribution given above.

p	f(p)
·016	1·26568
·037	2·46294
·054	3·11720
·070	3·52537
·083	3·73487
·096	3·85355
·109	3·89664
·122	3·87756
·135	3·80807
·148	3·69846
·162	3·54576
·177	3·35285
·192	3·13931
·209	2·88271
·227	2·60438
·247	2·29773
·271	1·9455
·300	1·5565
·337	1·13235
·394	·644941
·504	·16616

DONE
LIS
MAY2

```
1 DIM P[21], F[21]
5 FOR I = 1 TO 21
10 READ P[I]
15 LET F[I] = 90*P[I]*((1−P[I])↑8)
20 PRINT P[I], F[I]
25 NEXT I
100 DATA ·016, ·037, ·054, ·07, ·083, ·096
105 DATA ·109, ·122, ·135, ·148, ·162
110 DATA ·177, ·192, ·209, ·227, ·247, ·271, ·3, ·337, ·394, ·504
9999 END
```

Exhibit 5 The Posterior Distribution

The unconditional distribution of r:

$$P(r) = f_{Bb}(r/r', n', n)$$

$$= \frac{(r+1)!\,(108-r)!\,100!\,10!}{r!\,(100-r)!\,8!\,100!}$$

Mean $= E(r) = \dfrac{nr'}{n'} = \dfrac{200}{11} = 18$ This is used as an estimate for

the posterior distribution $f(P/E(r)) = 8.7681 \times 10^{22} p^{19}(1-p)^{99}$

P	$f(P/E(r))$
·016	3·41322E−32
·037	4·05069E−26
·054	1·07402E−23
·07	3·20375E−22
·083	2·29644E−21
·096	1·00842E−20
·109	3·05792E−20
·122	6·92903E−20
·135	1·23913E−19
·148	1·81913E−19
·162	2·28074E−19
·177	2·41439E−19
·192	2·16308E−19
·209	1·59953E−19
·227	9·68223E−20
·247	4·55111E−20
·271	1·43622E−20
·3	2·56719E−21
·337	1·76406E−22
·394	1·05268E−24
·504	1·67827E−30

```
DONE
LIS
1    DIM P[21]. F[21]
5    FOR I = 1 TO 21
10     READ P[I]
15     LET F[I] = 8.7681*10*22*P[I]↑19*(1−P[I])↑99
19     PRINT P[I]. F(I)
25   NEXT I
100   DATA ·016, ·037, ·054, ·07, ·083, ·096, ·109, ·122, ·135, ·148, ·162
110   DATA ·177, ·192, ·209, ·227, ·247, ·271, ·3, ·337, ·394, ·504
9999  END
NAM−MAY 3
```

Exhibit 6 Schematic for Test Market

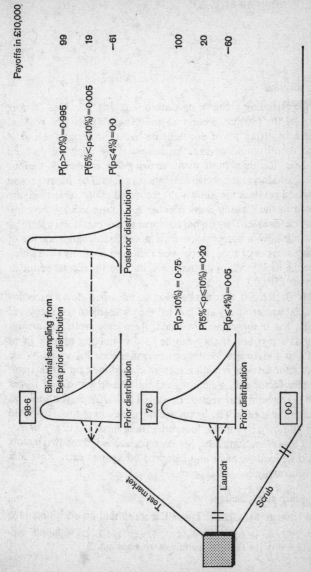

Payoffs in £10,000

99
19
−61

100
20
−60

P(p>10%)=0·995
P(5%<p≤10%)=0·005
P(p≤4%)=0·0

Posterior distribution

98·6

Binomial sampling from Beta prior distribution

Prior distribution

Test market

76

P(p>10%) = 0·75
P(5%<p≤10%)=0·20
P(p≤4%)=0·05

Prior distribution

Launch

0·0

Scrub

7 Hewitt Ingot Co.: Sale of Surplus Stocks
(Written as at 1972)*

Introduction

While attending a course on decision-making, Mr Alec Barton, head of the Casting Section at the Hewitt Ingot Co. realized that a recurring set of decisions he had to make at the end of each month could perhaps be improved by applying decision analysis. Residues from manufacturing the company's various metal products are reclaimed by ingotting. The ingotted and analysed residues are known as 'recovered melts', and these are stored in the Casting Section either for future use by the company or for sale. They do not conform to any particular specification but have a composition determined by a chance mixing of different types of alloy. Recovered melts are currently sold whenever the total stock of *all* materials, not just the recovered melts, exceeds £80,000.

Mr Barton felt that the decision to sell when stocks exceeded £80,000 was arbitrary and had led the company to sell recovered melts that it subsequently needed. Recovered melts are always sold at a loss but, if they can be used in making up new ingot melts to a given specification, they realize their full value. While this factor favours retaining each recovered melt until it is used, another factor works against this: the investment loss of 18 per cent per annum that accrues on stored melts. Thus, if it looks as though the melt will be in storage for a very long time, it should be sold now at a modest loss rather than incur the heavy investment loss later. Somehow, Mr Barton reasoned, these two factors could be made explicit and balanced off against each other in a decision analysis.

Approach to Consultant

In a letter to Mr Charles Durrell, a consultant on decision analy-

* This case was prepared by J. A. Morris and L. D. Phillips in conjunction with the Glacier Institute of Management.

sis, Mr Barton outlined the background of the project and asked him if a decision analysis would at least clarify the basis for keeping or selling the recovered melts. Here are relevant portions of the letter from Mr Barton.

(i)   Most of our metal residues are reclaimed by ingotting them. The ingotted and analysed residues are known as 'recovered melts'. They find an outlet in the make-up of new charges made to an exact specification by adding the appropriate amounts of pure metals.

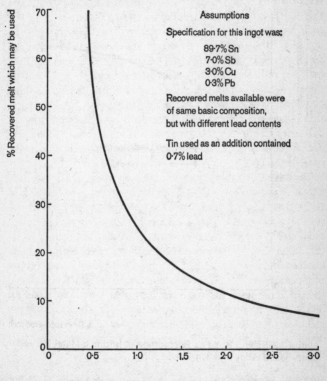

Assumptions

Specification for this ingot was:

89·7% Sn
7·0% Sb
3·0% Cu
0·3% Pb

Recovered melts available were of same basic composition, but with different lead contents

Tin used as an addition contained 0·7% lead

Figure 7.1 Illustration of the Way in which the Amount of Recovered Melt Permitted in a Tin-Based Alloy Varies with the Lead Content of the Recovered Melt

(ii) Recovered melts are more likely to be used if their degree of contamination is low, and more melt can be used in making up a new charge. This is shown in Figure 7.1. The bulk of our sales are of white metal recovered melts, and for these the degree of contamination is determined primarily by the proportion of lead in the melt. White metal is a term applied to any tin- or lead-based alloy.

(iii) The terms under which white metal is sold are very much affected by their composition. Figure 7.2 shows how the

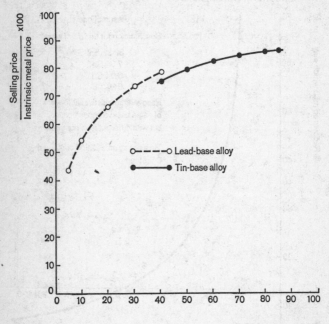

% Tin in recovered melt

Figure 7.2 Selling Price as Percentage of Intrinsic Metal Value for Lead-Based Alloy and Tin-Based Alloy

proportion of tin in the recovered melt affects the selling price. The selling price is expressed as a percentage of the intrinsic metal value (IMV), where the IMV is the total current market cost of the constituent metals.

(iv) The main criterion at present used in deciding whether or not a recovered melt should be sold is that the total stock level of all materials in the Casting Section should not exceed £80,000. It is likely that, with the present methods of operating, some selling of recovered melts will always be desirable. The melts sold will be those that are so contaminated that they are never likely to be used or, in the terms mentioned above, those where the sales loss is much less than the investment loss. However, many melts which might eventually be used profitably in new charges are, under the present policy of trimming down to £80,000, being sold off at a loss. Figure 7.3, based on the usage of

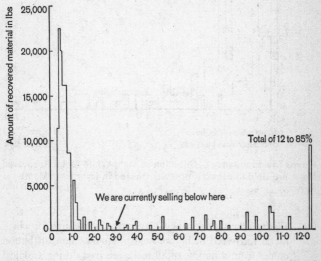

Figure 7.3 Usage of Recovered Melts in Making Ingots to Specification and by Selling Outside at a Loss

white-metal recovered melts last year, gives some evidence in support of this point. The situation has worsened since that time in that melts down to about 2½-per-cent lead are now being sold.

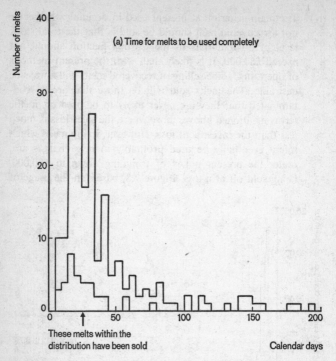

Figure 7.4a Frequency Distribution of Time White Metal Recovered Melts are Held in Stock. (For Melts Booked in Over Four-Month Period.)

(v) Figure 7.4a is a frequency distribution of the time for which metal recovered melts are held in stock. The distribution comes from a sample of all melts received during a typical four-month period, about 200 melts in all. The melts are not generally used at one stroke, but are taken from stock gradually. In other words, the stocks gradually decay. Figure 7.4b is a distribution showing the time taken for the stock level in each case to decay to half its original value. The figure has been prepared as a first attempt at estimating the real loss in investment value while the melt, or any part of it, is on the books. It would be an overestimate to base

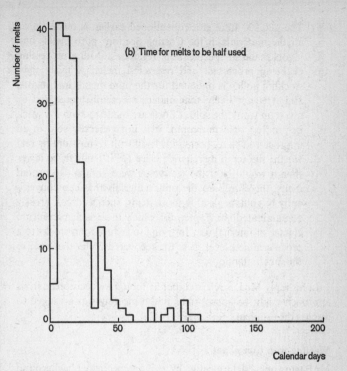

Figure 7.4b

the investment loss on the initial value of the melt and the time it took to dispose of it completely.

(vi) The most profitable way of disposing of recovered melts is to sell them as ingots to specification outside the company, for then they are got rid of completely. If used in ingots which are to be used within the company, a large portion of them return in the residue system. Sales of ingots outside the company are comparatively small. Overall profitability could possibly be increased by dropping the ingot prices to increase demand and so increase the opportunities for disposing of recovered melts.

(vii)   The £80,000 total stock mentioned earlier is made up of
        all the materials in the Costing Section: pure metals and
        ingots made to specification, residues awaiting processing
        or being processed, and recovered melts. A fairly tight
        stocking policy is operated for the pure metals and ingots,
        and it is not likely that materials recently purchased or
        made up would be sold. Efforts are made to keep the work
        in progress at a minimum. It is not generally sold in an
        unprocessed state, because it is difficult to measure its real
        worth; the scrap merchant's price for it tends to be lower
        than it would be if the real value were known. Recovered
        melts, therefore, are the only materials that can conveni-
        ently be sold, neglecting those items, such as dross, grossly
        contaminated swarf, etc., for which there is at present no
        chance of internal use. In trying to reduce total stocks to a
        predetermined level, it is the recovered melts that receive
        the most attention.

In his reply Mr Durrell said that he thought a decision analysis
approach might be appropriate, and a meeting was arranged to
discuss the problem.

Meeting with Consultant

Mr Barton opened the meeting by giving some further background
information:

'Requests for new ingots come both from other sections of our
own company and from outside customers. We make up a new
melt to the customer's specifications, and the composition is
optimal, in terms of minimizing our cost, because it is determined
by linear programming.

'Melts sold outside our company rarely come back as residue.
Those that do come back from our own company are sometimes
in contaminated form, and we have to make them back up into
the exact specifications. We do this by adding more pure materials.
Those that are left as we received them can be sold as recovered
melt, but we don't get their IMV. What we do get depends on
their tin content.'

'How often does a recovered melt that you have in store meet the precise specifications of a customer?' Mr Durrell was speaking.

'Very rarely', replied Mr Barton.

'What is the size and IMV of your most valuable melts in stock?' inquired Mr Durrell.

'About £1,000 to £1,500 per ton, and the melts are often in one-ton ingots'.

'And how many melts might be in stock at any one time?'

'About twenty to fifty.'

'Do you have any limitations on storage space?'

'Not really. I wouldn't worry about that because much more space is taken by our pure-metal stock than by the recovered melts. There's always space for the recovered melts.'

'Will the scrap dealer take any recovered melt you want to get rid of?'

'Yes, but he probably wouldn't bother to pick up just one or two tons. He would probably want at least four tons to make it worth the trouble. However, that's a policy I might persuade our buying office to change if you think it's worth it.'

'I'm not sure just now,' replied Mr Durrell. 'Let's get back to the recovered melts in stock. Can anything be gained by considering the ingots in combination when you decide to keep or sell them?'

'I don't see how. I have a separate record of each one showing the date when it was received, an analysis of its own composition, its weight when received, and the weight remaining at the end of each month.'

'When do you review your stocks of recovered melts?'

'At the end of each month. If total metal stocks are above £80,000 at the end of the month, I weed out the least promising recovered melts, the ones I'm afraid I'll have around for a long time with no occasion to use.'

'Tell me about trends in the metal market and how they affect your decisions.'

'I take these into account when I consider the present and future IMV of each melt, but I don't think fluctuations in the market are nearly as serious in influencing my decisions as the discrepancy between selling cost and IMV, or as the investment loss, at least for the alloys I'm mainly concerned with.'

'Can you give me an example of a recovered melt that you were absolutely sure you should keep, another which appeared utterly useless, and a third that you were uncertain about? Tell me also the I M V and sale price of each.'

Mr Barton produced as illustrative the three melts shown in the following table:

Melt No.	K62	J28	K81
Composition			
% Tin (Sn)	83·99	85·26	82·37
% Antimony (Sb)	10·28	7·68	7·82
% Copper (Cu)	5·21	4·33	3·87
% Lead (Pb)	0·52	2·73	5·94
Original weight	1 ton	1 ton	1 ton
Intrinsic value	£1,309	£1,300	£1,261
Sale price	£1,130	£1,131	£1,092
Decision	Keep	?	Sell

Issues for Discussion

(1) In what way do you feel decision analysis can contribute to solving Mr Barton's decision problem?

(2) Go as far as you can in solving Mr Barton's problem.

(3) A dynamic programming formulation does not yield an immediate solution. As alternative approaches try: (a) a simulation approach, or (b) simplifying the structure of the problem to fit the available dynamic programming algorithms.

(4) What decision should be made about melt J28?

References

Readers are referred to the following items:

FISHER, J. C., 'A class of Stochastic Investment Problems', *Operations Research*, Vol. 10, 1962.

BECKMANN, M., *Dynamic Programming and Economic Decisions*, Springer Verlag, Berlin, 1968.

WAGNER, H. M., *Principles of Operations Research*, Prentice-Hall, 1969.

The chapters relating to adaptive and dynamic programming in the latter two books are particularly relevant.

8 Property Redevelopment in Caracas: An Investment Decision
(Written as at 1970)

Introduction

The Board of one of the major Venezuelan banking organizations was facing the problem of how best to re-utilize the considerable property value of its main office building in Caracas. The building was an extremely fine, fifteen-year-old block, architecturally splendid and occupying a magnificent site in the city centre. But, quite simply, the organization had grown too big for these offices and a much larger site was being developed a little way out from the centre which would provide the necessary extra space and better facilities for the modern style of banking with its greater range of financial services, extensive computerization, etc.

As an alternative to selling the existing property outright in its present condition, the bank could keep the building as an investment and redevelop it as shops, apartments, offices, hotel, or some seemingly optimal mixture of these uses. Apart from these various configurations of space utilization, there were various structural changes which could be made to the building. Two extra floors could be added which, together with further modification, would increase the choice of possible space utilization configurations. A major reconstruction could also provide a more efficient utilization of the floor space, and a plan devised in 1967 had already been approved by the planning authorities. A more recent scheme submitted in 1969 had not yet been approved. However, with certain members of the Board having considerable influence in the city, the possibility of the plans being turned down was described as inconceivable.

The Options Available

At this stage, the Board decided to enlist the help of a consultant Mr R. B. Gale, to assist in analysing and resolving the problem. His first act was to construct a list of the possible options open to the bank.

After considering systematically the possible space utilization configurations for each structural possibility, a set of apparent investment options was drawn up and is displayed in Appendix 1. In Appendix 2 the various costs involved in each of these investment options are listed. Indemnification refers to the cost of evicting present tenants. In an attempt to take into account the uncertainty in the estimates of construction costs in present value terms, and in order to facilitate subsequent calculations, these costs were assessed in terms of a Normal distribution function. The subjectively assessed means and variances are shown in Appendix 2. The mean was assessed as the fiftieth percentile (or median), i.e. that value at which it was thought there was an equal chance of the cost being above or below.

The variance (or squared standard deviation) was estimated indirectly by assessing first the fifth percentile and the ninety-fifth percentile of the distribution. These two percentiles were assessed by using the standard artificial device of drawing one ball at random from an urn with either 5 per cent or 95 per cent red balls and estimating the construction cost at which the decision-maker would be indifferent as between going ahead with the construction or receiving a prize equal to that cost if the ball drawn is red. The difference between the two costs estimated in this way is approximately equal to 3·3 times the standard deviation.

At the same time Mr Gale extracted from the Board their subjective probability estimate of 0·9 that the 1969 plans would go through the planning authorities unimpeded.

Appendix 3 lists the various categories of space utilization, which are then used in Appendix 4 to evaluate the expected rent revenues from each option. With the intention of granting leases for the full twenty-year planning horizon, the main uncertain factor in revenue estimation is the degree of occupancy over the period. The subjectively assessed probability distributions for revenues were again approximated by the Normal distribution function, with means given by the expected values for rent revenues from Appendix 4, and variances assessed at one tenth of these expected mean values for each alternative, being a measure of the uncertainty about the occupancy rates.

The terminal value of each investment option proved the most difficult to estimate. Clearly in twenty years time the value of the property will depend not only upon the general trend in land prices, but also on how a potential buyer in twenty years time would assess the revenue possibilities of the property. A city like Caracas changes its character rapidly and, with many of the other large financial and commercial organizations also planning new headquarters outside the centre, there were already the signs of the city shifting its centre of gravity. Even if a new building on the 1969 code were constructed, the market value of the property in twenty years time would clearly have to be based solely upon its redevelopment potential. The Board finally agreed upon a terminal value of 6·5 million bolivars, in present day terms, with a variance of 4.

The Bank's Attitude towards NPV

A consideration persistently at the forefront of the Board's thinking is that of maintaining the company's image and customer goodwill. For this reason they would only be prepared to let the property out to prestige hoteliers and retailers. Hence in estimating the value of outright sale (Option 1), the need to find the right sort of buyer who would not pull it down immediately, but maintain it in first class condition and use it for highly respectable purposes, had to be taken into account. As a consequence the subjective probability distribution of the sale value was found to have the rather high variance of 1 against the mean of 6. Furthermore, many members of the Board had expressed strong opposition to those options which involved demolishing and redeveloping the existing building. Their argument, perhaps owing more to sentiment than economic reality, was that the building symbolized the immortal and impregnable security of the bank and that they should avoid even the slightest undertones of transience.

As a starting point, however, net present value (NPV) was considered to be an appropriate criterion with which to evaluate these investment options. The sums of money involved in any of the options were not considered to impose any strain on the bank's resources. The cost of capital was taken to be about 10 per cent, and the discount factor thus $1/\left(1+\dfrac{10}{100}\right)$ or 0·9091.

The NPV of rent revenues was easily obtained from the formula

$$R = 12r(1-d^{20})/(1-d)$$
$$= 113r$$

where R = NPV of rents over twenty years
r = rent revenue per month
d = discount factor (0·9091)

Since the sum of a number of independent Normal variables is itself distributed Normally, the NPV for each investment can be evaluated as a Normal distribution. Appendix 5 summarizes the mean and variance of the NPV for each investment option. In considering Option 17, the Board strongly favoured the idea of holding an equity interest in the department store. 4m. bolivars was being contemplated, which they assessed as an independent investment, to give an NPV, distributed Normally with a mean and variance of 3m.

The Board looked to Mr Gale for advice upon which of the seventeen options they should adopt. For each option the NPV, distributed Normally with specific means and variances, had been estimated and the problem was to determine the Board's attitude to risk and how they wished to trade off NPV mean against variance.

The Utility Evaluation

It was clear that some members of the Board evaluated risk as the probability of the NPV of the investment being less than zero. Clearly, in this case, the option with smallest risk would be that with the highest value of the quantity $\dfrac{\text{NPV mean}}{\text{NPV standard deviation}}$

Accordingly Mr Gale plotted a graph (shown in Figure 8.1) of NPV mean against NPV standard deviation for the seventeen options. By considering the line from the origin to each of the seventeen points, the highest ratio of mean to standard deviation is achieved by Option 2, all other options having a higher slope and hence a lower ratio.

Other members of the Board were evidently less conservative in their attitude towards risk. Several expressed a preference for Option 17, with its high expected return, despite the greater risk.

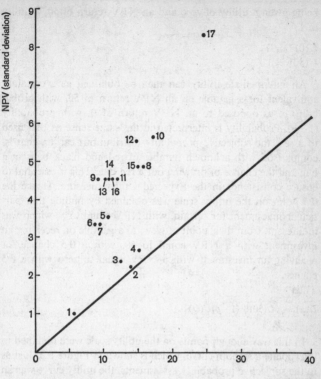

Figure 8.1 Mean and Standard Deviations of the Investment Options

The decision analyst realized, therefore, that it was necessary to evaluate more explicitly the Board's attitude to risk by constructing a corporate utility function for NPV.

A decision based upon expected utility would be a consistent one with respect to their overall preferences under uncertainty. A utility function over a range of NPV values could be obtained from responses to a set of artificial bets, similar to those used in the assessment of subjective probability. Since such a utility scale is arbitrary up to a linear transformation, the end points of the scale were conveniently established with an NPV return of 0 being given a utility of zero and an NPV return of 50, a utility of 1;

$$U(0) = 0$$
$$U(50) = 1$$

An intermediate utility can then be obtained as a certainty equivalent for a gamble on an NPV return of 50, with probability p, as opposed to an NPV return of 0, with probability $(1-p)$. Probability is interpreted in the same sense as that used to assess the subjective probability distributions earlier, that is, comparison with a known number of red and black balls in a bag and the chance of drawing out a red one. This is essential to ensure consistency in the Expected Utility measure. Hence the 0·5 point on the utility scale was obtained by finding that particular investment for certain, with NPV equal to x, which was indifferent, from their point of view, to a gamble on receiving an investment with a NPV equal to 50, with a 0·5 chance, or receiving an investment with a NPV equal to zero with a 0·5 chance.

Thus

$$U(x) = pU(50) + (1-p)U(O)$$
$$= p$$

In this way enough points on the utility scale were obtained to interpolate a smooth curve, which is shown in Figure 8.2. Just as in the subjective probability assessments, the utility curve was an aggregate from all the individuals on the Board. The derivation of a consensus involved considerable introspection and questioning of the initial divergences in opinion and, unfortunately, the final consensus may perhaps have been over-influenced by those members of the Board with the more persuasive personalities.

The Expected Utility (EU) principle involves evaluating, for each investment, the product of each possible NPV return with its associated probability. For investment i ($i = 1, 2, \ldots 17$)

$$EU_i = \int_{-\infty}^{+\infty} U(x)p_i(x)\, dx$$

where $p_i(x)$ for each investment is a Normal density function with appropriate mean μ_i, and standard deviation σ_i.

In order to avoid fitting a mathematical function to the utility curve and then evaluating the integral for each investment, advantage was taken of a well-known mathematical approximation

$$U(x) = U(\mu) + (x-\mu)U'(\mu) + \tfrac{1}{2}(x-\mu)^2 U''(\mu) \dots \tag{1}$$

where $U'(\mu)$ and $U''(\mu)$ represent first and second derivatives of the Utility function $U(x)$ evaluated at $x = \mu$. Hence taking the expectation of $U(x)$

$$E(U(x)) = U(\mu) + \tfrac{1}{2}\sigma^2 U''(\mu) + (\text{negligible terms}) \tag{2}$$

and therefore for investment i

$$EU_i = U(\mu_i) + \tfrac{1}{2}\sigma^2_i U''(\mu_i) \tag{3}$$

$U(\mu_i)$ can be read off directly from the utility function plotted in Figure 8.2. In Appendix 6, second differences of $U(x)$ are

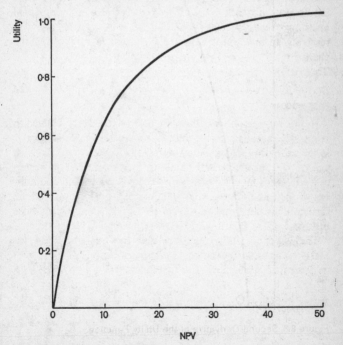

Figure 8.2 Utility Curve for NPV

113

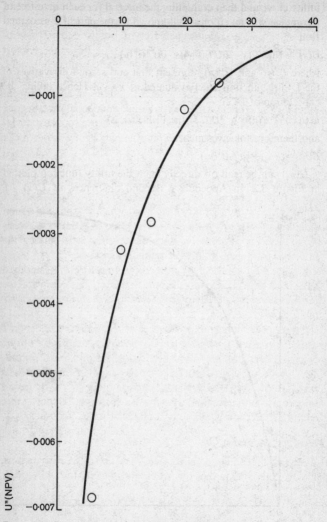

Figure 8.3 Second Derivative of the Utility Function

evaluated by first evaluating $U'(x)$, the gradient of the utility function at intermediate points, and then $U''(x)$, the gradient of the gradient at specific points on x. A curve of $U''(x)$ is plotted in Figure 8.3, as an interpolation of points derived in Appendix 6.

Using this approximation, EU_i can be easily evaluated for all i. It is, in practice, only necessary to evaluate those investments which are contained in the 'efficient' subset of all investment options. The efficient subset excludes all dominated investments, and an investment is dominated if it has a NPV standard deviation roughly equal to another, but a significantly lower mean NPV.

As investment Option 2 did not turn out to have the maximum expected utility, the decision analyst now had to advise the Board which approach was most valid. It was recognized that maximizing expected utility elucidated which investment option would be most consistent with the Board's own attitude to investment under uncertainty. It does nothing towards helping the Board to formulate what their attitude should be.

The method of using the ratio NPV (mean)/NPV (standard deviation) provided a very definite criterion, but one with the rather conservative basic interpretation of risk as the probability of a negative NPV.

Other, non-quantified, preferences of the Board, such as their desire to preserve the building and, through it, the Bank's image, if feasible, had moreover not been taken into account. Fortunately, such is the economic climate for commerce in Venezuela that, whilst the Government's taxation policies might be an important consideration in investment-planning in most other countries, taxation is blissfully negligible for the Venezuelans.

Issue for Discussion

Assuming that you were in Mr Gale's position, give, with reasons, the choice of option that you would recommend to the Board.

Appendix 1 The Set of Apparent Options

1 Sell the property in its present condition.
2 Retain and use as offices.
3 Retain and use as offices with slight modifications.
4 Add two floors and use as offices and retail shops.
5 As 4, with slight modifications.
6 As 5, but with apartments.
7 As 5, but incorporate an hotel.
8 Construct new building (1967 plan) for offices and retail shops.
9 As 8, but incorporating an hotel.
10 As 8, but with department store.
11 As 8, but with apartments.
12 As 8, but with just offices and department store.
13 Construct new building (1968 plan) for offices and retail shop.
14 As 13, but use for hotel.
15 As 13, but use for offices and department store.
16 As 13, but with apartments.
17 Construct new building (1970 plan) but with considerable expansion and use it for department store.

Appendix 2 Investment Costs*

Option	Facilities	Construction cost Mean	Construction cost Variance	Indemnification cost	Total cost Mean	Total cost Variance
1	−10·5			4·5	−6·0	1
2		1·55	0·1		1·55	0·1
3		4·53	0·8		4·53	0·8
4		6·90	2		6·9	2
5		8·85	7	4·5	13·35	7
6		8·20	6	4·5	12·7	6
7		8·35	6	4·5	12·85	6
8		14·80	17	4·5	19·3	17
9		13·70	15	4·5	18·2	15
10		16·45	25	4·5	20·95	25
11		13·72	15	4·5	18·22	15
12		16·00	24	4·5	20·5	24
13		13·87	15	4·5	18·37	15
14		13·79	15	4·5	18·29	15
15		14·70	17	4·5	19·2	17
16		13·69	15	4·5	18·19	15
17	10·3	25·80	64	4·5	40·6	64

* All units are million bolivars.

Appendix 3 Summary of Floor Space Categories

Code	Description
01	Class A office
02	Class B office
03	Class A office, new rentals
04	Class B office, new rentals
05	Class B office, existing rentals
A1	Class A apartment, 1970 plan
A2	Class A apartment, 1968 plan
A3	Class A apartment, existing building
H1	Class A hotel, 1970 plan
H2	Class A hotel, 1968 plan
H3	Class A hotel, existing building
D1	Class A department store, large
D2	Class A department store, medium
D3	Class A department store, small
R1	Class A retail, prime
R2	Class A retail, secondary
R3	Class A retail, mezzanine
R4	Class B retail, ground
R5	Class B retail, ground, existing rental
P	Parking space
U	Unusable space

Appendix 4 Rent Revenues*

Space code	Rent† per square metre	Option							
		2	3	4	5	6	7	8	9
O1	16							11,380	
O2	14·5			3,798	4,053				
O3	11·5	4,674	4,898		5,412				
O4	10	514	514	4,674		5,412	5,412		
O5	10			514					
A1	17·5								
A2	16					2,981			
A3	13								
H1	14								13,063
H2	13						3,803		
H3	11·5								
D1	19								
D2	19								
D3	19								
R1	27								
R2	22·5							911	
R3	16	118	432	118	2,756			300	
R4	13	2,324	2,324	2,324		2,756	2,756	1,246	
R5	13								
P	4·8	232	232	232	232	232	232	4,310	4,402
U	0								
Total rent revenue/month		83,500	97,000	140,000	157,000	136,000	140,000	256,000	190,000

* Figures in table denote the appropriate space availability in square metres.
† Rent is expressed in bolivars per month.

119

Rent Revenues (*contd*)

Space code	Rent per square metre	Option							
		10	11	12	13	14	15	16	17
O1	16							7,049	
O2	14·5		4,185	8,580	9,424		2,465		
O3	11·5								
O4	10								
O5	10								
A1	17·5		5,394						
A2	16							2,105	
A3	13								
H1	14					12,996			
H2	13								
H3	11·5								24,400
D1	19						10,171		
D2	19	14,018							
D3	19			6,390					
R1	27		720		1,176			1,246	
R2	22·5		240						
R3	16		1,014						
R4	13								
R5	13								
P	4·8	3,039	4,378	3,002	4,186	4,450	3,036	4,186	5,250
U	0								
Total rent revenue/month		285,000	210,000	276,000	200,000	202,000	250,000	202,000	495,000

Appendix 5 NPV Mean and Variance

Option	Rent (mean) (a)	Cost (mean) (b)	Resale (mean) (c)	Equity (mean) (d)	Total NPV Mean	Total NPV Variance
1		−6·00			6·00	1
2	9·43	1·55	6·5		14·38	5
3	10·96	4·53	6·5		12·93	6
4	15·82	6·9	6·5		15·42	7·5
5	17·74	13·35	6·5		10·89	13
6	15·37	12·70	6·5		9·17	11·5
7	15·82	12·85	6·5		9·47	11·5
8	28·92	19·30	6·5		16·12	24
9	21·40	18·20	6·5		9·70	21
10	32·20	20·95	6·5		17·75	32
11	23·70	18·22	6·5		11·98	21
12	31·20	20·50	6·5		17·20	31
13	22·60	18·37	6·5		10·73	21
14	20·80	18·29	6·5		11·01	21
15	28·20	19·20	6·5		15·50	24
16	22·80	18·20	6·5		11·10	21
17	55·90	40·60	6·5	3	24·80	71

(i) All units are million bolivars.
(ii) Final variance: sum of variances for rent, cost, resale, and equity.
(iii) NPV is net present value at the discount rate used (see text).
(iv) Mean NPV is equal to $(a)-(b)+(c)+(d)$

Appendix 6 Evaluation of the Second Differences of the Utility Function

NPV	U(NPV)	U'(NPV)	U''(NPV)
0	0		
		0·080	
5	0·40		−0·0068
		0·046	
10	0·63		−0·0032
		0·030	
15	0·78		−0·0028
		0·016	
20	0·86		−0·0012
		0·010	
25	0·91		−0·0008
		0·004	
30	0·96		

9 Aztech Electronics: Evaluation of Research and Development Projects
(Written as at 1972)

Background

Aztech Electronics is a comparatively large and well-established company with its principal activities in the micro-electronics industry. It is a subsidiary of an international electronics organization, but has considerable autonomy in its UK operations.

The main reason for undertaking research and development work is defined by corporate management as being the need to provide the principal base on which the long-term growth of the company can be developed. In operational terms this implies that research and development work has to achieve a sufficient level of profitability to maintain the future growth of the firm out of internally generated funds. It is not surprising, therefore, that the research and development work in the firm is applied in nature and oriented towards the development of both new and existing products.

Research and development is organized on a departmental basis with a manager appointed to direct its operations. The links between the managing director, the head of R & D, and the heads of the various sub-departments within R & D are close, and weekly management meetings at which the R & D manager and sub-managers are present are held. There has always been a special relationship between the R & D manager and the managing director because of the strategic importance of R & D work to the firm. Their joint philosophy is basically that, without good R & D, they might as well go out of business. This philosophy is offensive rather than defensive; R & D is there to develop new areas of technical competence in advance of competitors.

The research and development manager controls a skilled research staff, whose overall size is about 7 per cent of the total employment of the firm in all functional areas. He has a number of senior project engineers directly under him who are responsible for the day-to-day operations of the various projects which make up the research department's portfolio of projects. The process by which project ideas are generated within the firm is unsystematic, the search process for new project ideas being delegated to all the project engineers and sales engineers. In fact most project ideas are generated from the research and development staff with a number of improvements in design, i.e. applied design projects being suggested by production engineers. Sales engineers often stumble upon untapped market demands and are responsible for putting firms who want a special instrument designed and made in touch with the R & D manager. A few ideas come also from other sub-departments in the company; but the major source is the R & D laboratory itself.

The Handling of New Projects

The firm divides a new project idea once generated into four phases of research:

(i)   Investigation.
(ii) Laboratory Prototype.
(iii) Production Prototype.
(iv) Pilot Run.

The investigation phase is the most interesting and is the one discussed in this case, because it is at this phase that decisions about possible adoption of projects are made. It comprises three more or less separate stages which can be described as follows:

(a) Preliminary Product Survey

In this stage a broad definition of the technical features of the project is required. In the light of this definition a list of possible technical approaches for the product is drawn up and critical technical areas are identified and evaluated. A preliminary evaluation of the market for the eventual product and its likely costs is also made. This preliminary survey is generally carried out by the engineer who put forward the initial idea.

(b) Detailed Design Study

This presupposes a satisfactory outcome for the preliminary study. The outcome of the initial study is reviewed at a meeting of the R & D manager with the senior project engineers. A detailed study of possible project designs is then carried out by teams of research and design engineers to ascertain the design which is most feasible in terms of overcoming major technical problems at a given cost level.

(c) Project Proposal

Stage (b) is an essential prerequisite for (c). In (c) a complete technical specification is prepared for the project and, where possible, preliminary circuit diagrams are provided. The specification is accompanied by a formal market estimate, i.e. an evaluation of economic factors and a time schedule for the development project.

This detailed project proposal is most often carried out by a senior project engineer who coordinates the opinions of the project initiator and the research and design teams employed on the project.

The Second Stage of Evaluation

Once this initial review has been carried out by the project initiator, the project idea is passed on to the research manager for action. He generally convenes a meeting of his senior project engineers to evaluate the areas in which greater information about the feasibility of the project is needed. Once the areas are defined, a working party of research and design engineers is set up to evaluate the project in detail and this team is encouraged to maintain close liaison with the marketing, sales, production, and financial areas of the firm. The process of reviewing projects occurs regularly in the R & D department, and projects are formally reviewed as and when they are generated. One of the main elements of the formal review is the judgement of the potential worth of a proposed development in terms of financial criteria, such as the likely return on the R & D investment. The calculation of such criteria is not regarded as being the sole basis on which the decision to adopt a particular project is made. Occasionally overriding technical or other reasons influence decisions and alter the weighting given to financial evaluations. Nevertheless, financial criteria are given the greatest importance by the research and development manager in his project selection decision.

The Consideration of Ten Projects

Following the above principles, ten projects had recently come up for evaluation. Four senior project engineers made their separate assessments on whether each of these projects was worth investing in.

Project 1

One of a projected family of instruments for electronic measurement. The objective of pursuing the concept of the family of instruments was a result of a company plan to produce a range of test instruments in an area not previously exploited by the company. Market potential was considered by the company to be considerable and the expertise was available within the research and development laboratory to carry out the work.

Project 2

A complementary instrument to Project 1 produced to extend the product line.

Project 3

The final member of the first phase of a series of instruments defined by Projects 1, 2, and 3. The latter was produced to provide a complete measurement system for the customer and to provide training for existing engineers in the technical area before the launching of the second phase of this system of instruments. Again, market potential for the system was estimated to be considerable.

Project 4

A measurement instrument sponsored and planned by the laboratory management to follow on and replace an existing instrument. The modifications were designed to improve the capability and performance of the device. The market potential was thought to be large.

Project 5

A re-design of an existing instrument for a specific customer. The request for the research to be done emanated from the sales division who considered that the market offered was profitable to the company.

Project 6

An instrument specifically planned by the laboratory management to place the firm in a new area of electronic measurement. Again, the market was considered to be very large and the measurement area one with great long-term potential. As a result the project was felt to be a learning exercise to some extent as well as a profitable venture for the company and its technical staff.

Project 7

An electronic measurement instrument designed to meet known existing demand. Again a family of instruments was planned and in this case it is considered reasonable to view them as one, rather than three distinct projects. The idea for the project was generated within the laboratory.

Project 8

An instrument designed and planned to be used as a complementary instrument to an existing successful product marketed by the firm. The market for the instrument was thus considered to be steady but not great.

Project 9

An instrument designed as a result of technical 'fall-out' from the series of Projects 1 to 3. Considered to have a useful market potential and overall benefit for the firm.

Project 10

An instrument designed specifically to a special contract from a customer. Sales department considered the development would be extremely profitable for the firm, and the laboratory regarded the development work as being a fairly simple task.

The Evaluation of the Projects

As a first stage in the project evaluation, an analysis on a purely financial basis was carried out. The simulation approach was adopted since distributions of the internal rates of return (IRR)

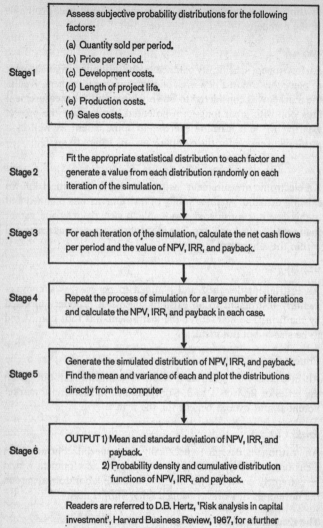

| Stage 1 | Assess subjective probability distributions for the following factors:

 (a) Quantity sold per period.
 (b) Price per period.
 (c) Development costs.
 (d) Length of project life.
 (e) Production costs.
 (f) Sales costs. |

| Stage 2 | Fit the appropriate statistical distribution to each factor and generate a value from each distribution randomly on each iteration of the simulation. |

| Stage 3 | For each iteration of the simulation, calculate the net cash flows per period and the value of NPV, IRR, and payback. |

| Stage 4 | Repeat the process of simulation for a large number of iterations and calculate the NPV, IRR, and payback in each case. |

| Stage 5 | Generate the simulated distribution of NPV, IRR, and payback. Find the mean and variance of each and plot the distributions directly from the computer |

| Stage 6 | OUTPUT 1) Mean and standard deviation of NPV, IRR, and payback.
 2) Probability density and cumulative distribution functions of NPV, IRR, and payback. |

Readers are referred to D.B. Hertz, 'Risk analysis in capital investment', Harvard Business Review, 1967, for a further discussion of this program.

Figure 9.1 The Risk Simulation Program

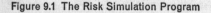

could easily be obtained in addition to those of net present value (NPV). A structural flow chart for the procedure is shown in Figure 9.1. Net cash flows per period were assumed to be independent and assessed as Normal probability distributions. Each of the four decision-makers made assessments under various assumptions of the project's life. Tables 1, 2, 3, and 4 summarize the financial assessments obtained from each decision-maker. It will be noted that the four decision-makers did not make assessments of all the projects concerned.

However, for reasons mentioned earlier, such a purely financial analysis was considered too narrow in view of the other objectives which the company set for its research and development programmes. The complete set of objectives that were considered relevant by Aztech were as follows:

(i)   Profitability.
(ii)   Growth and diversity of the product line.
(iii) Offensive research mounted to anticipate competition.
(iv)   Increased market share.
(v)   Maintained technical capability.
(vi)   Increase in firm's reputation and image.
(vii) Provision of interesting research work to maintain engineer creativity.

A practical way of dealing with these objectives is via the Churchman–Ackoff model, the basis of which is described in the Appendix. Each decision-maker is asked to give the projects some weight (between 0 and 1) according to the extent to which it satisfies each of the seven objectives given above. He is also required to give a weight (again between 0 and 1) to each of the seven objectives, assessing its importance and subject to the restriction that the sum of the weights for all the seven objectives must be 1. A weighted objective score is obtained as described in the Appendix, and these scores for the ten projects, over the seven objectives, from each of the four decision-makers, are summarized in Table 9.5. Table 9.6 gives the decision-makers' consensus estimates of the costs anticipated for each project.

As there were no immediate capital-rationing constraints, the primary problem was not to determine which of the projects should be undertaken, but to assess the worth of each project as

Table 9.1 Decision-Maker 1

Project	Length of life (years)	IRR (%) Mean (SD)	Payback (Years) Mean (SD)	NPV at 10% (£) Mean (SD)	NPV at 15% (£) Mean (SD)	NPV at 20% (£) Mean (SD)	NPV at 25% (£) Mean (SD)
1	7	126·40 (3·95)	2·53 (0·04)	224750·25 (7735·27)	177891·06 (6273·63)	142163·16 (5183·60)	114536·31 (4320·83)
2	4		1·70 (0·08)	241574·81 (207515·5)	204928·81 (18364·87)	174653·19 (16398·62)	149435·62 (14734·66)
2	5	140·23 (12·68)	1·68 (0·07)	287407·25 (21601·30)	241748·12 (18795·00)	204526·37 (16795·46)	173893·94 (14393·09)
2	6	138·82 (13·31)	1·70 (0·08)	307244·75 (21980·25)	256668·00 (19343·36)	215831·25 (17182·66)	182512·06 (15371·20)
3	7	242·27 (8·50)	2·25 (0·02)	847168·69 (27414·72)	679080·06 (22103·64)	550615·00 (13148·94)	451069·50 (15077·94)
4	7	61·18 (3·37)	3·40 (0·09)	30023·27 (1573·22)	22404·97 (1321·43)	16711·98 (1119·31)	12407·14 (964·13)
5	5	79·19 (3·98)	2·70 (0·05)	103578·75 (7232·00)	82895·75 (6128·98)	66458·50 (5225·32)	53278·18 (4489·47)
5	6	85·92 (3·63)	2·72 (0·08)	143929·81 (7545·21)	114851·12 (6303·92)	90930·81 (5358·06)	72630·19 (4592·86)
5	7	92·30 (3·33)	2·72 (0·08)	196037·75 (8536·27)	153748·25 (6994·76)	121417·06 (5839·66)	96383·62 (4939·21)
8	3	>500	1·07	332566·69	298725·56	269625·50	244434·06

8		(0·01)	(21526·84)	(19312·31)	(17424·93)	(15827·29)
4	>500	1·07	442844·25	390890·56	347231·00	310231·25
		(0·01)	(24098·02)	(21349·54)	(14034·38)	(17125·23)
10	506·50	1·21	207502·81	183480·50	163081·12	145635·50
3	(31·47)	(0·02)	(8913·48)	(8002·81)	(7171·43)	(6435·10)
10	526·50	1·21	350226·00	302973·31	263877·62	231254·50
4	(22·72)	(0·01)	(12544·00)	(10752·00)	(9413·00)	(8245·32)

Table 9.2 Decision-Maker 2

Project	Length of life (years)	IRR (%) Mean (SD)	Payback (Years) Mean (SD)	NPV at 10% (£) Mean (SD)	NPV at 15% (£) Mean (SD)	NPV at 20% (£) Mean (SD)	NPV at 25% (£) Mean (SD)
2	3	41·62 (15·34)	2·06 (0·23)	26018·14 (12486·37)	19787·99 (11304·25)	14579·86 (10286·72)	10202·60 (9404·92)
2	4	77·60 (13·53)	1·99 (0·15)	79432·81 (15143·40)	65463·97 (13451·82)	53921·07 (12035·66)	44312·50 (10837·70)
2	5	90·38 (11·73)	2·00 (0·15)	126438·06 (16084·64)	103774·00 (14105·86)	85424·94 (12485·58)	70432·00 (11142·25)
2	6	97·86 (11·77)	1·99 (0·15)	172256·19 (19827·09)	139829·06 (17093·75)	114128·62 (14897·57)	93528·50 (13122·81)
2	7	36·97 (1·89)	4·35 (0·09)	96308·12 (7548·20)	64575·75 (5944·60)	41542·98 (4777·04)	24644·39 (3917·91)
3	7	233·75 (6·65)	2·28 (0·02)	782198·87 (27117·88)	627294·50 (21951·91)	508785·87 (18074·76)	416867·19 (15077·94)
4	7	178·46 (8·05)	2·43 (0·03)	129682·19 (4132·34)	103423·44 (3349·47)	83377·06 (2793·66)	67863·94 (2343·66)
5	7	92·35 (3·34)	2·65 (0·08)	227217·06 (8804·82)	177733·19 (7248·40)	140046·27 (6084·37)	110968·37 (5158·25)

Table 9.3 Decision-Maker 3

Project	Length of life (years)	IRR (%) Mean (SD)	Payback (Years) Mean (SD)	NPV at 10% (£) Mean (SD)	NPV at 15% (£) Mean (SD)	NPV at 20% (£) Mean (SD)	NPV at 25% (£) Mean (SD)
6	4	40·59 (16·93)	3·03 (0·32)	177776·81 (102635·19)	131073·44 (88110·25)	93835·56 (76202·87)	63949·38 (66354·44)
6	5	56·92 (10·78)	3·00 (0·26)	361974·50 (89755·25)	278682·62 (76475·44)	213245·81 (65711·44)	161390·37 (56898·52)
6	6	64·11 (10·03)	2·97 (0·27)	525625·25 (106396·25)	404049·44 (89080·62)	310412·00 (75410·12)	237517·19 (64440·73)
6	7	67·18 (9·69)	3·01 (0·28)	671624·62 (125638·06)	510521·87 (103083·12)	389032·50 (85735·60)	296221·06 (72133·37)
6	8	101·44 (5·49)	2·59 (0·12)	1498318·00 (89117·37)	1157742·00 (72675·12)	903978·00 (60124·58)	711898·00 (50450·84)

Table 9.4 Decision-Maker 4

Project	Length of life (years)	IRR (%) Mean (SD)	Payback (Years) Mean (SD)	NPV at 10% (£) Mean (SD)	NPV at 15% (£) Mean (SD)	NPV at 20% (£) Mean (SD)	NPV at 25% (£) Mean (SD)
2 (run 1)*	3	−4·08 (18·14)	2·87 (0·16)	−11219·93 (14719·70)	−14719·54 (12968·23)	−16259·61 (11495·42)	−18394·79 (10247·88)
2 (run 2)	3	−2·20 (5·91)	2·96 (0·07)	−11040·69 (5422·57)	−14022·69 (4437·91)	−16391·54 (4523·93)	−18272·62 (4167·37)
2 (run 1)*	4	12·37 (11·74)	3·22 (0·5)	3014·63 (12825·58)	−2198·90 (11289·07)	−6387·83 (10000·25)	−9714·16 (8911·28)
2 (run 2)	4	12·63 (4·99)	3·14 (0·24)	2894·92 (5373·44)	−2364·92 (5170·44)	−6513·96 (4372·76)	−9843·42 (4018·66)
2 (run 1)*	5	15·13 (11·10)	3·49 (0·74)	6497·69 (13557·10)	404·28 (11893·68)	−4419·11 (10502·84)	−8256·21 (9330·85)
2 (run 2)	5	16·96 (4·81)	3·23 (0·28)	943·49 (5118·80)	−4114·52 (4579·48)	−8148·22 (4126·45)	−11376·18 (3742·35)
6	5	105·30 (6·65)	2·57 (0·07)	881574·37 (81321·00)	713935·87 (67848·69)	581270·87 (57180·34)	475253·94 (48656·84)
6	6	107·89 (5·92)	2·58 (0·07)	1036561·37 (79089·06)	832361·12 (65442·43)	672758·25 (54782·20)	546645·44 (46323·98)
6	7	107·94 (6·62)	2·58 (0·07)	1109396·00 (92040·44)	884228·44 (76304·69)	710084·44 (63947·75)	573755·25 (54106·92)
7	3	4·07	2·88	−5680·40	−9542·51	−12639·83	−15127·84

		(7·68)	(0·12)	(7785·22)	(6672·34)	(5988·22)	(5408·16)
7	5	28·26	2·91	47110·27	33957·37	23515·70	15162·16
		(5·80)	(0·17)	(9928·05)	(8625·91)	(7563·82)	(6688·96)
7	6	27·49	3·28	31532·95	19676·25	10373·49	3026·40
		(5·44)	(0·20)	(9708·32)	(8494·93)	(7500·94)	(6678·80)
10	3	26·74	2·53	12655·69	7652·96	3547·03	161·34
		(14·67)	(0·20)	(10654·57)	(9902·01)	(9256·92)	(8698·27)
10	4	54·30	2·51	50789·48	39636·50	30578·67	23169·31
		(14·70)	(0·18)	(11301·14)	(10354·18)	(9572·68)	(8918·00)
10	5	61·31	2·51	70762·37	55647·80	43543·93	23766·78
		(12·29)	(0·18)	(10233·80)	(9288·67)	(8527·65)	(7904·26)

* The table gives for project 2 the simulation results from two runs of the same model. This provides some guidelines for the accuracy of the results from simulation experiments.

Notes on Tables 9.1 to 9.4
(a) SD = standard deviation.
(b) IRR = internal rates of return.
(c) NPV = net present value.

Table 9.5 Project Scores over Seven Objectives

	*DM 1		DM 2		DM 3		DM 4	
Project	Score	Rank	Score	Rank	Score	Rank	Score	Rank
1	28·34	5 =	42·59	2	30·40	5	39·68	4 =
2	23·51	7	31·03	7	35·15	3	19·93	8
3	38·91	2	35·34	4	37·31	2	41·85	3
4	18·35	8	32·14	6	—		57·54	2
5	28·34	5 =	39·64	3	—		39·68	4 =
6	31·20	4	28·88	8	31·62	4	38·28	6
7	—		12·29	10	40·11	1	16·26	9
8	44·57	1	44·25	1	—		58·60	1
9	—		34·97	5	23·09	6	—	
10	35·95	3	23·51	9	—		24·92	7

* DM = Decision-Maker. Scores expressed as percentages.

Table 9.6 Estimated Costs for Each Project

Project	1	2	3	4	5	6	7	8	9	10
Cost (£0000)	2·76	2·74	2·72	1·05	0·7	3·66	1·11	1·53	2·54	3·77

a R & D investment. Aztech's process of project evaluation had left them with the task of reconciling on the one hand the alternative approaches to assessing project worth and on the other hand the differing views of the four senior project engineers.

Issues for Discussion

(1) Which of the ten projects discussed should be accepted? Which of the financial criteria discussed (i.e. NPV, IRR, payback) are appropriate for decision-making in this context?

(2) If there were a financial constraint of £50,000 on the amount that Aztech could spend on R & D, would the selection problem be altered? If so, in what respects?

(3) Has Aztech's process of project evaluation introduced decision-making problems which would be avoided with an alternative project review structure?

(4) How would you allow for risk in the selection of projects, either with or without a financial constraint?

Appendix
Churchman–Ackoff Model for Multi-Dimensional Objectives

The following is a concise description of the Churchman–Ackoff model for evaluating a set of projects on a basis of multiple objectives.

1. Suppose that, at some moment in time, the decision-maker assigns a relevant set of objectives $(O_1 \ldots, O_n)$ for his decision problem.
2. Suppose also that he has a number of alternative research projects $(R_1 \ldots, R_k)$ which need to be evaluated.
3. The decision-maker then constructs a $(k \times n)$ matrix with alternative projects as rows and objectives as columns.

$$
\begin{array}{cccc}
 & O_1 & \ldots & O_n \\
\text{Weights} & W_1 & \ldots & W_n \\
\hline
R_1 & & \ldots & \\
\cdot & & \ldots & \\
\cdot & & \ldots & \\
\cdot & & \ldots & \\
R_k & & \ldots &
\end{array} = (M)
$$

4. The cells in the matrix are assigned values between 0 and 1 according to the extent to which each R_i satisfies each of the objectives.
5. The decision-maker is also asked to estimate a positive weight W_i to each objective subject to the restriction that

$$\sum_{i=1}^{n} W_i = 1$$

in order to establish the priority between objectives. Let W be the $(n \times 1)$ column vector of weights.
6. A weighted objective score is then calculated for each project R_i by obtaining the $(k \times 1)$ column vector S by matrix multiplication, i.e.

$$S = M \times W$$
$$(k \times 1) = (k \times n)(n \times 1)$$

This weighted objective score is the criterion by which preliminary project decisions should be made.

Readers are referred to C. W. Churchman, *Introduction to Operations Research*, Wiley, 1951, for fuller details of this multidimensional model.

10   J. Sainsbury Ltd: Bidding for Contraband Butter

(Written as at August 1968)

Introduction

In an attempt to control the imports of butter, the UK Board of Trade imposed a quota scheme to run over twelve months from 1 April 1967. The total import quota was to be 470,000 tons for the whole period, out of which Australia and New Zealand were assigned just over half. After only a few months of operation, it became clear that the objective of the scheme was being frustrated by a sharp rise in the imports of 'near butters'. From November 1967, therefore, all licences for butter oil, butter fat, resolidified butter and dehydrated or anhydrous butter were revoked; except in special circumstances such as in the case of goods for re-export. Sweetfat was not included in this revocation of import licences.

With another avenue now closed, the more determined butter importers chose to adopt less respectable means of quota evasion. Particularly popular, by all accounts, was the use of a sweetfat cover to import prohibited quantities of butter. Notwithstanding the ingenuity of these not-so-altruistic butter importers, Her Majesty's Customs and Excise maintained its traditional vigilance and made this importing procedure one of considerable risk. Extracts from the *London Gazette* of 26 March 1968 indicated that 500 tons of such 'moonshine' butter, improperly described as sweetfat, had been impounded at the Port of London.

Subsequently, in August 1968, J. Sainsbury Ltd received an invitation to tender for this haul of butter. The chief buyer was aware of the circumstances of the seizure but naturally wished to obtain more information, particularly regarding the country of origin, its quality, and especially some estimate of the relative amounts of butter and sweetfat in the cartons. Sweetfat was much cheaper than butter on the open market, but the bid price had to be a composite one for the mixture of both the butter and the sweetfat. Representatives of any of the companies invited to tender were allowed, if they wished, to inspect a sample of the haul chosen by a Customs Officer at random from the deep-freeze, prior to submitting their bid. They were required to submit a sealed bid by 16 September 1968. The companies did not have to tender for all of the 500 tons, and the Customs and Excise did not bind themselves to accepting the highest bid; but, *ceteris paribus*, the chances of being awarded the goods would be higher, the greater the amount tendered for. It was felt, moreover, that the Customs and Excise preference was for disposing of the haul between several tenders if the minimum price tendered in this composite set of bids were greater than the highest bid offered for the whole lot.

The Chief Buyer's Analysis

250 of the 20,000 cartons had already been withdrawn from the deep freeze when Sainsbury's Chief Buyer arrived. He was given ten of these, without choice, to inspect. From a laboratory analysis the sample was found to contain 80-per-cent butter (20-per-cent sweetfat) and considered to be of satisfactory quality. However, it was considered that, because of the small size of the sample, very little could be said about the proportion of butter in the full 500-ton haul and, furthermore, nothing could be gleaned from the markings on the cartons.

Some inspired reasoning on the part of the Chief Buyer was able to provide a more compelling indication. He argued that one could subjectively infer the proportion of butter by considering the geometry of the way in which the butter and the sweetfat were packed. If the hold of the ship contained both butter and sweetfat, then either the sweetfat would be separated on a pallet above the butter, or it would be separated by pallets on all sides. Given the rough dimensions of the hold and the assumption that such an importer would not conceivably take such risks if the butter proportion were less than 50 per cent, the Chief Buyer made subjective assessments of the following probabilities:

% Sweetfat	15	20	25	30	35	40	45
Probability	0·05	0·2	0·4	0·2	0·05	0·05	0·05

Insofar as this opportunity to tender for butter was to be

considered completely extraordinary business, and therefore unbudgeted for, a purely marginal approach to costing the bid could be justified. Moreover, continuing this line of reasoning further, with the company having found itself in the position of having to bid or not, the administrative expenses involved in this decision-making should also not enter into the costing. The only significant marginal costs (apart from the bid price itself) would be stockholding costs, if necessary, and a miscellaneous (mainly inspection) cost of about £5 per ton. The stockholding costs per ton of butter and sweetfat were assessed respectively at £1 and £2 per week. The average stockholding time for a ton of sweetfat would be about two weeks.

. The weekly demand for this type of butter was, at the time, fairly stable; being assessed by the marketing men for the period in which it would be used at:

Demand (tons/week)	70	80	90	100
Probability	0·1	0·5	0·2	0·2

The Chief Buyer then estimated the likely buying price for Sainsbury Ltd of similar butter pertaining at the time when they might get hold of the consignment as follows:

Butter price (£/ton)	200	220	240	260	280	300
Probability	0·05	0·1	0·1	0·2	0·5	0·05

Similarly, the buying price of sweetfat at the time when Sainsbury might obtain the consignment was assessed as follows:

Sweetfat Price (£/ton)	110	130	150	170	190	210
Probability	0·05	0·4	0·2	0·2	0·1	0·05

Competition from Other Bidders

The chief buyer also had to face the most complex aspect of the whole problem: that of considering his pricing strategy in relation to the competitive nature of the tender. Through his contacts in the trade, he knew that there were four or five other large companies, like Sainsbury's in the running, who would have similar costs and who would most likely be thinking along the same lines. Also, there would doubtless be a larger number of smaller companies appearing who, it was recognized, generally had higher marginal costs, and, with weekly demands being significantly smaller, would be unlikely to bid for the whole tender.

The competitors were accordingly classified into two main sets: the Large Company (LC) set and the Small Company (SC) set. With no other indication of how the other LC competitors assessed the value of the consignment, the assumption of symmetry was made as a starting point. Hence Sainsbury's estimate of the value of the consignment was also their best estimate of how the other competitors evaluated the haul. It was suggested that the LC competitors would typically like to expect a margin of 20 per cent in this sort of business, with a risk of making a marginal loss of less than 5 per cent.

Still assuming symmetry of cost concepts, an assessment was then made on the possible upward shift in this postulated base price due to competitive out-thinking behaviour. Out-thinking behaviour results from the realization that a competitor's typical approach is that expected from him by the other competitors, and therefore represents his attempt to out-wit the others by bidding at a slightly higher price. The possible shifts due to such causes were estimated as follows:

Upward shift from typical base price due to out-thinking (£/ton)	5	10	15	20
Subjective probability	0·5	0·2	0·2	0·1

Finally, relaxing the symmetry assumption to take account of the uncertainty in the postulated base price, it was thought that the LC-set average cost concept might be distributed about Sainsbury's estimate as follows:

LC cost-concept variability (£/ton)	−10	−5	0	+5	+10
Subjective probability	0·05	0·2	0·5	0·2	0·05

Hence the average LC bid was conceived as being the summation of natural tendency, out-thinking shift and cost-concept variability. Having evaluated the average LC bid price subjective probability distribution in this way, it was necessary to consider the uncertainty in the number of such LC competitors. It was decided that the number of LC competitors could be approximated by a Poisson process, with a mean of 3. From a computational point, this is extremely convenient since, if b_i is Sainsbury's probability of being beaten by an average LC competitor at bid price 'i' then Sainsbury's probability of winning with bid 'i', taking into account the probabilities of all possible numbers of competitors, is given by $\exp(-3b_i)$.

Of the smaller companies, all that could be said was that their prices were likely to be very widely spread, with some taking optimistically long odds on low bids; but most, it was thought, might see their best chance in bidding at their weekly demand to avoid stockholding costs and thereby hoping that, if many did likewise, they would make up a sufficiently attractive bid in combination for the Customs and Excise to prefer to split up the haul. Many, it was suggested, might well collaborate to this end.

Issue for Discussion

On the basis of this information and analysis, what bid would you recommend Sainsbury's to make?

Acknowledgement

We are grateful to Messrs J. Sainsbury Ltd, not only for their patient cooperation, but also for allowing the undisguised publication of the case.

11 Whernside Construction Ltd: The Development of a Strategy for Repetitive Competitive Bidding
(Written as at 1973)

Introduction

The Whernside Construction Co. operates a world-wide spread of such construction and development activities as civil engineering, private housing, property development, building, dredging, mining, mechanical engineering, foundation engineering, and the manufacture of concrete products.

Table 11.1 indicates how one London firm of Investment Analysts were evaluating Whernsides in December 1972.

Table 11.1

Activities	Turnover £m.	Profit £m.
UK Contracting	40	0·7
Housebuilding	17	1·5
Property	2	0·8
Rental income		0·65
Concrete products	4	0·4
Mining	4	0·5
Dredging	4	0·45
Overseas		
Australia	18	0·925
Others	32	1·775
Totals	121	7·7

The company is highly geared with interest charges taking up about £1·2m. of this £7·7m. estimated pre-tax profit.

Contracting is evidently the major activity and something like 25 per cent of this £40m. UK contracting turnover is accountable to fixed-price tendering. The difficulties and risks involved with fixed-price-tendering activities are magnified considerably in such a period of high inflation. So cautious had most of the contractors become in 1972 that some 1½ per cent per month was being incorporated into the costing of these fixed-price tenders purely in an attempt to cover expected cost escalation. Most of this fixed-price tendering is associated with public-works engineering.

The larger, longer-term projects such as motorways and hospitals do, however, have a built-in cost-escalation clause. For this reason, and because the larger projects are less competitive with fewer companies being able to take on the tasks, Whernside prefers to concentrate on these major activities. The smaller contracts tend to become too competitive, particularly as a large number of the house-builders with heavy capital requirements often come into the running for purely cash-flow reasons.

The profitability of contracting is clearly very low. House-building profits, however, were expected to continue at their high level at least until 1974. Property profits were regarded by Whernside as a recurring item of about £1m. per year. As a proportion of total profits, their house-building and property profits are only about a half of the other main house-builders. But, whilst Whernside is clearly not making as much out of the current housing boom as some of the other major contractors, in the longer term, with the UK house-building industry subject to such severe downturns, it has been argued that it might be unwise to increase the proportion of house-building activities.

The contracts for British Rail concrete railway-sleepers and some open-cast coal mining are among many substantial longer-term contracts. The company also has a considerable international dimension to hedge against downturns in the home market. But, whilst the organization has considerable status, the Board are well aware that one slip in their profits' record could be the end of Whernside Construction Ltd as an independent organization. The performance of the Contracting Division in this context is particularly worrying. The crucial and persistent problem is that of improving the profits from the competitive bidding for fixed-price tendering.

One way of dealing with such a problem is to avoid it. One of the other major construction companies was recently reported in the financial press as feeling very pleased at having eliminated fixed-price tendering out of its operations completely. Alternatively one can set about constructing and applying a model of the bidding process.

Bidding Process Model

Concentrating on the competitive aspect of bidding, the first generation of models proposed was essentially game-theoretic, developing directly from the work of von Neumann and Morgenstern (1944). Although these models generally describe the bidding process quite well (Christenson, 1965, managed to develop a satisfactory game-theoretic model of the bidding process for US Corporate Securities), they can be criticized for their weak equilibrium solutions. From a prescriptive point of view, there appeared little incentive to pursue such strategies of low profitability.

The requirement, then, was for some method of prescribing reasonably good non-equilibrium solutions. Friedman (1956), adopting a decision-theoretic approach, managed to formulate a more prescriptively acceptable model. In decision theory, the game is not so much conceived against Hostile Opponents as against Natural Uncertainty. A subjective probability distribution is assessed over the range of possible bids of an 'average' competitor. A commonly made assumption is that the number of such average competitors can be satisfactorily described by a Poisson distribution of known parameter.

With a subjective distribution function $F(B)$ over the range of 'average' bids (B), where the protagonist bids at $B = b$, his probability of being beaten in a lowest-bidder-wins game is $F(b)$. If the number of competitors bidding follows a Poisson parameter λ, then the probability of the protagonist winning at bid $B = b$ is $\exp(-\lambda F(b))$. Using the expected-monetary-value criterion, one should thus select that value of b which maximizes

$$(b-c) \exp(-\lambda F(b))$$

where c = estimated cost. (See the Appendix for a full derivation of this formula.)

Historical Bidding Data

When historical data are available on the bidding behaviour of the previous tenders, an empirical distribution can replace the purely subjective assessments. Friedman suggested using the frequency distribution of $\dfrac{\text{competitor's bid}}{\text{protagonist's estimated cost}}$ as a means of reconciling the previous tenders to a common base suitable for prescriptive purposes. The resulting distribution is effectively one of an 'average' competitor's mark-up on the protagonist's estimated cost. By using estimated cost, and not actual cost, as the denominator the method is pragmatically very prescriptive since actual cost is, of course, not known until the contract has been won and completed and any biases in cost-estimation *vis-à-vis* the competitors will implicitly be incorporated into the distribution.

Some data have been collected on Whernside's tendering for construction contracts over the previous five years, and is displayed in Figure 11.1.

The task of assembling a satisfactory set of data is much more difficult in the UK than in, for example, the US, where details of tenders submitted are made public afterwards. In order to build up the frequency distribution of $\frac{\text{bid price}}{\text{Whernside's estimated cost}}$ Whernside had to persuade the various competitors to reveal their bids. They only achieved a 50-per-cent success rate and the sample of 107 tenders represents only about a quarter of the number of serious bids Whernside submitted over the period.

With such a frequency distribution being intended to represent an 'average' competitor's probability distribution over mark-up, considerable care must be taken in using it to prescribe a bidding strategy. The various sources of bias must be recognized clearly and fully.

Whilst every attempt was made to include only the serious bids in the sample, it was inevitable that many 'cover prices' were included as well. A cover price is one in which a contractor submits a bid which he knows will be beaten (by ringing up a friendly competitor and asking for a 'safe cover') in order to preserve good relations with the customer offering the contract. The mini-peak in the right-hand tail of the curve probably represents cover prices. It has been estimated that about one in six of the tenders submitted are cover prices.

Another particularly important source of bias arises from the way in which the data are an aggregation of the 107 sets of bids over a period of six years. In any one tender, the set of bids will generally be clustered together closer than the variance of the Friedman curve suggests. Particular characteristics of the contract

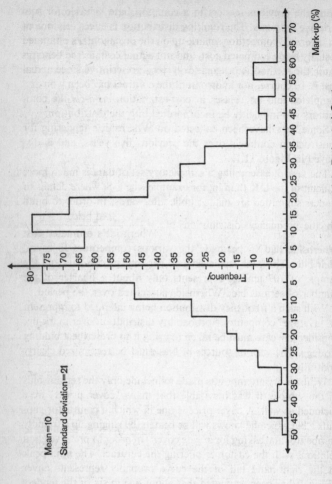

Mean = 10
Standard deviation = 21

Figure 11.1 Competitor's Price Mark-Up on Whernside's Estimated Costs

being offered for tender might be such that all the bidders would only consider it worthwhile (because of risk factors, utility considerations, etc.) at a relatively higher mark-up, etc. Also, over the period, there may have been various cyclic and trend factors influencing the average mark-up. The problem is shown diagrammatically in Figure 11.2.

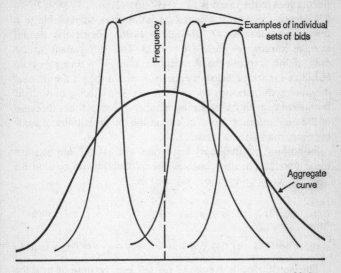

Figure 11.2 Combination of Mark-Ups

Unfortunately the data were not classified according to relevant characteristics of the tender and so nothing could be done to retrieve the first type of situation; but an annually computed average mark-up is available as shown.

Year	1966	1967	1968	1969	1970	1971	Total
Number of tenders	12	10	12	17	20	36	107
Average mark-up (%)	9	8	12	8	8	14	10

If the assumption is made that the annual variance is approximately constant with the annual mean fluctuating over the six years, the average annual variance about the mean (as opposed to the six-year average variance given by the frequency distribution) can be established.

The six-year aggregate curve has mean 10 and variance 441. Hence the sum of the squared deviations $= 107 \times 441 = 47,187$. But the sum of the squared deviations attributable to annual fluctuations in the mean is $12 \times (1)^2 + 10 \times (2)^2 + \ldots + 36 \times (4)^2 = 824$ Hence the sum of squared deviations not attributable to a fluctuating mean is $47,187 - 824 = 46,363$ Hence the annual average variance $= 46,363/107 = 433$ This adjustment would only slightly improve the chances of winning if Whernsides were to bid at a mark-up below the mean; it would reduce the chances of winning at mark-ups above the mean. The effect is only slight but increases with an increasing number of competitors (because of the multiplication 'rule' of evaluating the probability of beating more than one competitor).

Smoothing the frequency histogram, and taking into account these two bias factors enables the probability of beating an 'average' competitor to be evaluated as:

Mark-up (%)	0	1	2	3	4	5	6	7	8	9	10	15	20
Probability of winning	0·68	0·66	0·63	0·61	0·58	0·56	0·53	0·51	0·48	0·46	0·44	0·33	0·24

The distribution is skewed to the left and, because of this, the median is about 7 compared with a mean of 10. It may well be that this is due to the inclusion of cover prices in the distribution. It is not essential to remove these cover-price tenders, providing that the cover prices are then included in the set of competitors when considering bidding strategy; if cover prices are eliminated from the distribution, only serious bidders are considered as competitors.

Although the time-series data on the annual means had little effect on reducing the annual average variance, it gives some indication of a possible trend and cycle effect in the annual competitors mean mark-up. Whether a significant inference can be made from a sample of six is doubtful, but the important point is that the frequency distribution obtained, being an aggregate of the last six years, is really centred in time at a point three years ago. Clearly some forecast of the current mean is required, and the previous time-series, albeit of any six items, can give some indication of this.

Developing an overall strategy for the repetitive bidding process is effectively one of establishing a perspective in the prescription of individual bids such that the long-term accrued benefits are in some sense optimal. In more concrete terms such a strategy should provide guidelines for the calculation of a particular bid such that the bidding policy will maximize long-term objectives whilst giving the necessary freedom for consideration of the special individual characteristics of any particular bid.

The Formulation of a Bid

As a start, the mark-up model of Friedman could be used to determine a bid level for Whernside. The empirically derived probabilities of winning at particular levels of mark-up are established from the frequency histogram. The average number of competitors per tender was six. The assumption of a Poisson distribution over the number of competitors per tender is not an unreasonable one and this would allow the usual calculation of that mark-up which would be optimal under the EMV criterion. The model is clearly very simplistic, however.

It is generally accepted that contracts are won not so much through sophisticated mark-up models, but through the chance under-estimation of the costs likely to be involved in the project. This is one of the main reasons for the low profitability of fixed-price tendering. Whernside revealed that their average mark-up over estimated costs for the last five years was about 7 per cent. The actual profit on contracting for 1972 has already been seen to fall considerably short of this.

It has been argued that the Friedman model does not take explicit account of the uncertainty in the protagonists' cost estimates. In particular, the assertion that the probability of beating an average competitor at a given mark-up, when the probability of beating any one is equal to p, is given by p^n has been dismissed as false by those who argue that the independence requirements are not satisfied. If the protagonist has beaten one competitor, they argue, he is more likely to beat the next than if he had not beaten the first, since it is then more probable that his cost estimate is biased.

If a perfectly symmetrical repetitive game between a protagonist and n competitors, where each have the same cost estimate and mark-up policy distribution, is envisaged, then because of symmetry the protagonist's chance of winning is clearly $1/(1+n)$. In fact, on the data collected, Whernside's success probability was found to be 0.16.

Data are available with which to construct a cost-estimate distribution about actual cost and this could be incorporated into a model suitably formulated.

The Utility Function

The expected-monetary-value criterion may not adequately reflect Whernside's attitude to risk. It is important to examine the significance of using expected utility as a criterion. The construction of a corporate utility curve as a consensus of the policy determining individuals' utility curves poses difficult aggregation problems. Alternatively one can attempt to prescribe the sort of utility curve that Whernside should have, in view of how they should rationally confront the risks involved in repetitive competitive bidding.

The bulk of Whernside's profits is made up from non-contracting activities which are very profitable and are sufficient in themselves to carry the overheads of the group and satisfy shareholders. However, Whernside does not want to appear unprofitable in their contracting and, since they have enough other long-term contracts for satisficing purposes, it might be postulated that they should attach a small utility to winning contracts at low margins, particularly with the uncertainty in the estimation of costs. In the light of the overall low profitability of contracting, any margin above 8 per cent might be considered good. Such reasoning would suggest a utility function along the lines of Figure 11.3.

The basic strategy so far postulated is to treat each bid on a marginal basis, maximizing expected utility whilst allowing corporate overheads to be effectively carried by the more profitable long-term operations in the group. Corporate overheads are probably relatively small compared with the costs directly involved in the type of larger contracts that Whernside

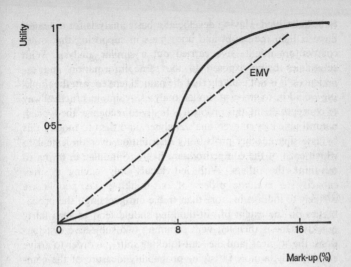

Figure 11.3 Suggested Utility Function

go in for. Thus, with fixed-price tendering becoming a decreasingly important aspect of the industry, treating each bid on a marginal basis and maximizing expected utility would appear to be a rational strategy. A marginal analysis presupposes, however, that subsequent decisions will be unaffected by the outcome of a given bid. In other words, if a particular bid is lost, this will not affect the utility function for the next tender. If losing a bid causes greater caution next time, and this would certainly be the case if there were overheads for example to apportion, then perhaps one should re-think the overall annual strategy in the light of having to expect to win at least a certain number of bids a year. Thus one has some sort of quantity constraint, which could be the apportioning of a given overheads total, or the maintenance of company prestige, etc. In such cases a better strategic basis might be to use a criterion such as finding that mark-up for which the chance of winning less than a certain number of tenders per year is below some defined critical figure.

By strategy, a certain frame of reference is implied with which to approach each bid as it comes along; obviously each bid will then be considered in its own right in formulating the actual bid to be submitted. Having developed a basic analysis for a tender, there is then the doubt and uneasiness in supposing that other competitors might have carried out a similar analysis. With companies being exposed to the same information and experiences, it is not unlikely that the natural tendency in the thinking would be to arrive at similar analyses. A simple, practical way of conceptualizing this problem is firstly to recognize the typical, natural tendency in everyone's analyses, and then to modify this by assessing another probability distribution over the extent to which each of the competitors are likely to indulge in trying to out-think the others. With individuals only having a small capacity to evaluate orders of out-thinking (i.e. people are unlikely to indulge in more than treble out-guessing), the probabilities on the extent of out-thinking should tend to zero fairly quickly. One is then left with summing two subjective distributions, the 'typical' and the 'out-thinking shift', in order to arrive at, hopefully, a more satisfying probability measure of the competitors' behaviour.

The low profitability of competitive bidding has long been recognized as bad for the industry. For this reason many government authorities who care, particularly some European ones, have been adopting a tendering system which has been much advocated by theorists and is gradually now becoming more accepted. Quite simply it is one where the contract is awarded to the second-lowest bidder. This has fascinating implications. Not least, it avoids the theoretical infinite regress in out-thinking leading to minimum profit margins. As part of the overall development of Whernside's bidding strategy, flexibility to cope with such second-lowest-bidder-wins situations should be incorporated.

Whernside's excellent connections with the financial institutions and their ability to arrange adequate finance has always been one of their strengths when tendering. Even though non-price considerations are not generally very significant in UK contracting, Whernside's proven management ability, its reputation for project planning, and efficiency were particularly good assets not only at home, but especially when tendering for overseas contracts.

Another positive factor to encourage optimistic long-term

planning is that UK government contracts tend to be offered on a serial basis such that a contractor can reasonably expect to receive subsequent follow-up contracts after winning a contract which is part of some overall government programme (e.g. motorways, airports, hospitals, etc.).

Issues for Discussion

(1) Discuss the appropriateness of the Friedman model as a means of developing a bidding strategy for Whernside.
(2) How far are simulation techniques likely to be useful as an alternative to analytic formulations in the determination of bidding strategies?
(3) Evidence is presented in the case regarding inaccuracies in cost estimates for contracts. Suggest procedures for obtaining improved cost estimates in the future.
(4) Do you agree with the suggestions made about competitive behaviour in the case, i.e. 'typical shift' and 'out-thinking shift'? Do you consider that they are operationally meaningful?
(5) What information systems might a contracting manager in Whernside have to set up in order to implement any of the decision-theoretic models suggested in the case?
(6) Is Whernside's suggested utility function realistic?

References

CHRISTENSON, C., *Strategic Aspects of Competitive Bidding for Corporate Securities*, Harvard University, 1965.

FRIEDMAN, L., 'A Competitive Bidding Strategy'. *Operations Research*, Vol. 4, 1956.

VON NEUMANN, J., and MORGENSTERN, O., *The Theory of Games and Economic Behavior*, Princeton University, 1944.

Appendix
Derivation of Bidding Formula

B is the variable representing an average competitor's bid for a particular sub-set of the total population of competitors, and $f(b)$ is the assessed probability distribution on B. In the lowest-bidder-wins game against one competitor, $F(b)$ is the probability

155

of the competitor beating the protagonist. With n competitors the probability of all n competitors beating the protagonist is

$$P(n, bt, p) = (F(b))^n$$

If the probability of M competitors arriving is represented by a Poisson process with parameter λ (where λ is the expected number of competitors), then the probability that M equals the specific value m is

$$P(M = m) = \lambda^m \exp(-\lambda)/m!$$

Hence

$$P(n, bt, p/M = m) = \binom{m}{n}(F(b))^n(1-F(b))^{m-n}\lambda^m \exp(-\lambda)/m!$$

and therefore

$$P(n, bt, p) = \sum_{m=0}^{\infty} \binom{m}{n}(F(b))^n(1-F(b))^{m-n}\lambda^m \exp(-\lambda)/m!$$

Thus

$$
\begin{aligned}
P(O, bt, p) &= \sum_{m=0}^{\infty} ((1-F(b))\lambda)^m \exp(-\lambda)/m! \\
&= \exp(\lambda(1-F(b)) \exp(-\lambda) \\
&= \exp(-\lambda F(b))
\end{aligned}
$$

Appendix A
Unit Normal Distribution

x	$f_N(x)$	$F_N(x)$	x	$f_N(x)$	$F_N(x)$
0·00	0·3989	0·5000	1·75	0·0863	0·9599
0·05	0·3984	0·5199	1·80	0·0790	0·9641
0·10	0·3970	0·5398	1·85	0·0721	0·9678
0·15	0·3945	0·5596	1·90	0·0656	0·9713
0·20	0·3910	0·5793	1·95	0·0596	0·9744
0·25	0·3867	0·5987	2·00	0·0540	0·9772
0·30	0·3814	0·6179	2·05	0·0488	0·9798
0·35	0·3752	0·6368	2·10	0·0440	0·9821
0·40	0·3683	0·6554	2·15	0·0396	0·9842
0·45	0·3605	0·6736	2·20	0·0355	0·9861
0·50	0·3521	0·6915	2·25	0·0317	0·9878
0·55	0·3429	0·7088	2·30	0·0283	0·9893
0·60	0·3332	0·7257	2·35	0·0252	0·9906
0·65	0·3230	0·7422	2·40	0·0224	0·9918
0·70	0·3123	0·7580	2·45	0·0198	0·9929
0·75	0·3011	0·7734	2·50	0·0175	0·9938
0·80	0·2897	0·7881	2·55	0·0154	0·9946
0·85	0·2780	0·8023	2·60	0·0136	0·9953
0·90	0·2661	0·8159	2·65	0·0119	0·9960
0·95	0·2541	0·8289	2·70	0·0104	0·9965
1·00	0·2420	0·8413	2·75	0·0091	0·9970
1·05	0·2299	0·8531	2·80	0·0079	0·9974
1·10	0·2179	0·8643	2·85	0·0069	0·9978
1·15	0·2059	0·8749	2·90	0·0060	0·9981
1·20	0·1942	0·8849	2·95	0·0051	0·9984
1·25	0·1826	0·8944	3·00	0·0044	0·9987
1·30	0·1714	0·9032	3·10	0·0033	0·9990
1·35	0·1604	0·9115	3·20	0·0024	0·9993
1·40	0·1497	0·9192	3·30	0·0017	0·9995
1·45	0·1394	0·9265	3·40	0·0012	0·9997
1·50	0·1295	0·9332	3·50	0·0009	0·99977
1·55	0·1200	0·9394	3·60	0·0006	0·99984

x	$f_N(x)$	$F_N(x)$	x	$f_N(x)$	$F_N(x)$
1·60	0·1109	0·9452	3·70	0·0004	0·99989
1·65	0·1023	0·9505	3·80	0·0003	0·99993
1·70	0·0940	0·9554	3·90	0·0002	0·99995
			4·00	0·0001	0·99997

The functions tabulated are

$$f_N(x) = \frac{1}{\sqrt{(2\pi)}} e^{-x^2/2} \text{ and } F_N(x) = \int_{-\infty}^{x} f_N(x)dx$$

Note on Appendices B and C

If the percentage rate of interest involved is r, and the number of years is n, then the value of 1 payable in n years given in Appendix B is

$$\frac{1}{\left(1+\dfrac{r}{100}\right)^n} \tag{1}$$

Such an amount, accumulated at r per cent for n years will then be precisely equal to 1.

Appendix C gives the value now of the sum of 1 payable at the end of each of the next n years. Thus, from formula (1) above the value for n equal to three will be

$$\frac{1}{\left(1+\dfrac{r}{100}\right)} + \frac{1}{\left(1+\dfrac{r}{100}\right)^2} + \frac{1}{\left(1+\dfrac{r}{100}\right)^3} \tag{2}$$

This is alternatively the amount that must be available now to pay the sum of 1 at the end of one, two, and three years respectively, leaving no capital remaining at the end of the three years.

Appendix B The Present Value of 1

| | | | | | Percentage | | | | | |
Year	1	2	3	4	5	6	7	8	9	10
1	0·990099	0·980392	0·970874	0·961538	0·952381	0·943396	0·934579	0·925926	0·917431	0·909091
2	0·980296	0·961169	0·942596	0·924556	0·907029	0·889996	0·873439	0·857339	0·841680	0·826446
3	0·970590	0·942322	0·915142	0·888996	0·863838	0·839619	0·816298	0·793832	0·772183	0·751315
4	0·960980	0·923845	0·888487	0·854804	0·822702	0·792094	0·762895	0·735030	0·708425	0·683013
5	0·951466	0·905731	0·862609	0·821927	0·783526	0·747258	0·712986	0·680583	0·649931	0·620921
6	0·942045	0·887971	0·837484	0·790315	0·746215	0·704961	0·666342	0·630170	0·596267	0·564474
7	0·932718	0·870560	0·813092	0·759918	0·710681	0·665057	0·622750	0·583490	0·547034	0·513158
8	0·923483	0·853490	0·789409	0·730690	0·676839	0·627412	0·582009	0·540269	0·501866	0·466507
9	0·914340	0·836755	0·766417	0·702587	0·644609	0·591898	0·543934	0·500249	0·460428	0·424098
10	0·905287	0·820348	0·744094	0·675564	0·613913	0·558395	0·508349	0·463193	0·422411	0·385543
11	0·896324	0·804263	0·722421	0·649581	0·584679	0·526788	0·475093	0·428883	0·387533	0·350494
12	0·887449	0·788493	0·701380	0·624597	0·556837	0·496969	0·444012	0·397114	0·355535	0·318631
13	0·878663	0·773033	0·680951	0·600574	0·530321	0·468839	0·414964	0·367698	0·326179	0·289664
14	0·869963	0·757875	0·661118	0·577475	0·505068	0·442301	0·387817	0·340461	0·299246	0·263331
15	0·861349	0·743015	0·641862	0·555265	0·481017	0·417265	0·362446	0·315242	0·274538	0·239392
16	0·852821	0·728446	0·623167	0·533908	0·458112	0·393646	0·338735	0·291890	0·251870	0·217629
17	0·844377	0·714163	0·605016	0·513373	0·436297	0·371364	0·316574	0·270269	0·231073	0·197845
18	0·836017	0·700159	0·587395	0·493628	0·415521	0·350344	0·295864	0·250249	0·211994	0·179859
19	0·827740	0·686431	0·570286	0·474642	0·395734	0·330513	0·276508	0·231712	0·194490	0·163508
20	0·819544	0·672971	0·553676	0·456387	0·376889	0·311805	0·258419	0·214548	0·178431	0·140644

Year	11	12	13	14	Percentage 15	16	17	18	19	20
1	0·900901	0·892857	0·884956	0·877193	0·869565	0·862069	0·854701	0·847458	0·840336	0·833333
2	0·811622	0·797194	0·783147	0·769468	0·756144	0·743163	0·730514	0·718184	0·706165	0·694444
3	0·731191	0·711780	0·693050	0·674972	0·657516	0·640658	0·624371	0·608631	0·593416	0·578704
4	0·658731	0·635518	0·613319	0·592080	0·571753	0·552291	0·533650	0·515789	0·498669	0·482253
5	0·593451	0·567427	0·542760	0·519369	0·497177	0·476113	0·456111	0·437109	0·419049	0·401878
6	0·534641	0·506631	0·480319	0·455587	0·432328	0·410442	0·389839	0·370432	0·352142	0·334898
7	0·481658	0·452349	0·425061	0·399637	0·375937	0·353830	0·333195	0·313925	0·295918	0·279082
8	0·433926	0·403883	0·376160	0·350559	0·326902	0·305025	0·284782	0·266038	0·248671	0·232568
9	0·390925	0·360610	0·332885	0·307508	0·284262	0·262953	0·243404	0·225456	0·208967	0·193807
10	0·352184	0·321973	0·294588	0·269744	0·247185	0·226684	0·208037	0·191064	0·175602	0·161506
11	0·317283	0·287476	0·260698	0·236617	0·214943	0·195417	0·177810	0·161919	0·147565	0·134588
12	0·285841	0·256675	0·230706	0·207559	0·186907	0·168463	0·151974	0·137220	0·124004	0·112157
13	0·257514	0·229174	0·204165	0·182069	0·162528	0·145227	0·129892	0·116288	0·104205	0·093464
14	0·231995	0·204620	0·180677	0·159710	0·141329	0·125195	0·111019	0·098549	0·087567	0·077887
15	0·209004	0·182696	0·159891	0·140096	0·122894	0·107927	0·094888	0·083516	0·073586	0·064905
16	0·188292	0·163122	0·141496	0·122892	0·106865	0·093041	0·081101	0·070776	0·061837	0·054088
17	0·169633	0·145644	0·125218	0·107800	0·092926	0·080207	0·069317	0·059980	0·051964	0·045073
18	0·152822	0·130040	0·110812	0·094561	0·080805	0·069144	0·059245	0·050830	0·043667	0·037561
19	0·137678	0·116107	0·098054	0·082948	0·070265	0·059607	0·050637	0·043077	0·036695	0·031301
20	0·124034	0·103667	0·086782	0·072762	0·061100	0·051385	0·043280	0·036506	0·030836	0·026064

Year	21	22	23	24	Percentage 25	26	27	28	29	30
1	0·826446	0·819672	0·813008	0·806452	0·800000	0·793651	0·787402	0·781250	0·775194	0·769231
2	0·683013	0·671862	0·660982	0·650354	0·640000	0·629882	0·620001	0·610352	0·600925	0·591716
3	0·564474	0·550707	0·537384	0·524187	0·512000	0·499906	0·488190	0·476837	0·465834	0·455166
4	0·466507	0·451399	0·436897	0·422974	0·409600	0·396751	0·384402	0·372529	0·361111	0·350128
5	0·385543	0·369999	0·355201	0·341108	0·327680	0·314882	0·302678	0·291038	0·279931	0·269329
6	0·318631	0·303278	0·288781	0·275087	0·262144	0·249906	0·238329	0·227374	0·217001	0·207176
7	0·263331	0·248589	0·234782	0·221844	0·209715	0·198338	0·187661	0·177636	0·168218	0·159366
8	0·217629	0·203761	0·190879	0·178907	0·167772	0·157411	0·147765	0·138778	0·130401	0·122589
9	0·179859	0·167017	0·155187	0·144280	0·134218	0·124930	0·116350	0·108420	0·101086	0·094300
10	0·148644	0·136899	0·126168	0·116354	0·107374	0·099150	0·091614	0·084703	0·078362	0·072538
11	0·122846	0·112213	0·102576	0·093834	0·085899	0·078691	0·072137	0·066174	0·060745	0·055799
12	0·101526	0·091978	0·083395	0·075673	0·068719	0·062453	0·056801	0·051699	0·047089	0·042922
13	0·083905	0·075391	0·067801	0·061026	0·054976	0·049566	0·044725	0·040390	0·036503	0·033017
14	0·069343	0·061796	0·055122	0·049215	0·043980	0·039338	0·035217	0·031554	0·028297	0·025398
15	0·057309	0·050653	0·044815	0·039689	0·035184	0·031221	0·027730	0·024652	0·021936	0·019537
16	0·047362	0·041519	0·036435	0·032008	0·028147	0·024778	0·021834	0·019259	0·017005	0·015028
17	0·039143	0·034032	0·029622	0·025813	0·022518	0·019665	0·017192	0·015046	0·013162	0·011560
18	0·032349	0·027895	0·024083	0·020817	0·018014	0·015607	0·013537	0·011755	0·010218	0·008892
19	0·026735	0·022865	0·019580	0·016788	0·014412	0·012387	0·010659	0·009184	0·007921	0·006840
20	0·022095	0·018741	0·015918	0·013538	0·011529	0·009831	0·008393	0·007175	0·006141	0·005262

Appendix C The Present Value of 1 per annum

Year	1	2	3	4	5	6	7	8	9	10
					Percentage					
1	0·990099	0·980392	0·970874	0·961538	0·952381	0·943396	0·934579	0·925926	0·917431	0·909091
2	1·97040	1·94156	1·91347	1·88609	1·85941	1·83339	1·80802	1·78326	1·75911	1·73554
3	2·94099	2·88388	2·82861	2·77509	2·72325	2·67301	2·62432	2·57710	2·53129	2·48685
4	3·90197	3·80773	3·71710	3·62990	3·54595	3·46511	3·38721	3·31213	3·23972	3·16987
5	4·85343	4·71346	4·57971	4·45182	4·32948	4·21236	4·10020	3·99271	3·88965	3·79079
6	5·79548	5·60143	5·41719	5·24214	5·07569	4·91732	4·76654	4·62288	4·48592	4·35526
7	6·72819	6·47199	6·23028	6·00205	5·78637	5·58238	5·38929	5·20637	5·03295	4·86842
8	7·65168	7·32548	7·01969	6·73274	6·46321	6·20979	5·97130	5·74664	5·53482	5·33493
9	8·56602	8·16224	7·78611	7·43533	7·10782	6·80169	6·51523	6·24689	5·99525	5·75902
10	9·47130	8·98259	8·53020	8·11090	7·72173	7·36009	7·02358	6·71008	6·41766	6·14457
11	10·3676	9·78685	9·25262	8·76048	8·30641	7·88687	7·49867	7·13896	6·80519	6·49506
12	11·2551	10·5753	9·95400	9·38507	8·86325	8·38384	7·94269	7·53608	7·16073	6·81369
13	12·1337	11·3484	10·6350	9·98565	9·39357	8·85268	8·35765	7·90378	7·48690	7·10336
14	13·0037	12·1062	11·2961	10·5631	9·89864	9·29498	8·74547	8·24424	7·78615	7·36669
15	13·8651	12·8493	11·9379	11·1184	10·3797	9·71225	9·10791	8·55948	8·06069	7·60608
16	14·7179	13·5777	12·5611	11·6523	10·8378	10·1059	9·44665	8·85137	8·31256	7·82371
17	15·5623	14·2919	13·1661	12·1657	11·2741	10·4773	9·76322	9·12164	8·54363	8·02155
18	16·3983	14·9920	13·7535	12·6593	11·6896	10·8267	10·0591	9·37189	8·75563	8·20141
19	17·2260	15·6785	14·3238	13·1339	12·0853	11·1581	10·3356	9·60360	8·95011	8·36492
20	18·0456	16·3514	14·8775	13·5903	12·4622	11·4699	10·5940	9·81815	9·12855	8·51356

Year	11	12	13	14	15	Percentage 16	17	18	19	20
1	0·900901	0·892857	0·884956	0·877193	0·869565	0·862069	0·854701	0·847458	0·840336	0·833333
2	1·71252	1·69005	1·66810	1·64666	1·62571	1·60523	1·58521	1·56564	1·54650	1·52778
3	2·44371	2·40183	2·36115	2·32163	2·28323	2·24589	2·20958	2·17427	2·13992	2·10648
4	3·10245	3·03735	2·97447	2·91371	2·85498	2·79818	2·74324	2·69006	2·63859	2·58873
5	3·69590	3·60478	3·51723	3·43308	3·35216	3·27429	3·19935	3·12717	3·05763	2·99061
6	4·23054	4·11141	3·99755	3·88867	3·78448	3·68474	3·58918	3·49760	3·40978	3·32551
7	4·71220	4·56376	4·42261	4·28830	4·16042	4·03857	3·92238	3·81153	3·70570	3·60459
8	5·14612	4·96764	4·79877	4·63886	4·48732	4·34359	4·20716	4·07757	3·95437	3·83716
9	5·53705	5·32825	5·13166	4·94637	4·77158	4·60654	4·45057	4·30302	4·16333	4·03097
10	5·88923	5·65022	5·42624	5·21612	5·01877	4·83323	4·63860	4·49409	4·33893	4·19247
11	6·20652	5·93770	5·68694	5·45273	5·23371	5·02864	4·83641	4·65601	4·48650	4·32706
12	6·49236	6·19437	5·91765	5·66029	5·42062	5·19711	4·98839	4·79322	4·61050	4·43922
13	6·74987	6·42355	6·12181	5·84236	5·58315	5·34233	5·11828	4·90951	4·71471	4·53268
14	6·98187	6·62817	6·30249	6·00207	5·72448	5·46753	5·22930	5·00806	4·80228	4·61057
15	7·19087	6·81086	6·46238	6·14217	5·84737	5·57546	5·32419	5·09158	4·87586	4·67547
16	7·37916	6·97399	6·60388	6·26506	5·95423	5·66850	5·40529	5·16235	4·93770	4·72956
17	7·54879	7·11963	6·72909	6·37286	6·04716	5·74870	5·47461	5·22230	4·98966	4·77463
18	7·70162	7·24967	6·83991	6·46742	6·12797	5·81785	5·53385	5·27316	5·03333	4·81219
19	7·83929	7·36578	6·93797	6·55037	6·19823	5·87746	5·58449	5·31624	5·07003	4·84350
20	7·96333	7·46944	7·02475	6·62313	6·25933	5·92884	5·62777	5·35275	5·10086	4·86958

163

Year	Percentage									
	21	22	23	24	25	26	27	28	29	30
1	0·826446	0·819672	0·813008	0·806452	0·800000	0·793651	0·787402	0·781250	0·775194	0·769231
2	1·50946	1·49153	1·47399	1·45682	1·44000	1·42353	1·40740	1·39160	1·37612	1·36095
3	2·07393	2·04224	2·01137	1·98130	1·95200	1·92344	1·89559	1·86844	1·84195	1·81611
4	2·54044	2·49364	2·44827	2·40428	2·36160	2·32019	2·27999	2·24097	2·20306	2·16624
5	2·92598	2·86364	2·80347	2·74538	2·68928	2·63507	2·58267	2·53201	2·48300	2·43557
6	3·24462	3·16692	3·09225	3·02047	2·95142	2·88498	2·82100	2·75938	2·70000	2·64275
7	3·50795	3·41551	3·32704	3·24232	3·16114	3·08331	3·00866	2·93702	2·86821	2·80211
8	3·72558	3·61927	3·51792	3·42122	3·32891	3·24073	3·15643	3·07579	2·99862	2·92470
9	3·90543	3·78628	3·67310	3·56550	3·46313	3·36566	3·27278	3·18421	3·09970	3·01900
10	4·05408	3·92318	3·79927	3·68186	3·57050	3·46481	3·36439	3·26892	3·17806	3·09154
11	4·17692	4·03540	3·90185	3·77569	3·65640	3·54350	3·43653	3·33509	3·23881	3·14734
12	4·27845	4·12737	3·98524	3·85136	3·72512	3·60595	3·49333	3·38679	3·28590	3·19026
13	4·36235	4·20277	4·05304	3·91239	3·78010	3·65552	3·53806	3·42718	3·32240	3·22328
14	4·43170	4·26456	4·10816	3·96160	3·82408	3·69485	3·57327	3·45873	3·35070	3·24867
15	4·48901	4·31522	4·15298	4·00129	3·85926	3·72607	3·60100	3·48339	3·37264	3·26821
16	4·53637	4·35673	4·18941	4·03330	3·88741	3·75085	3·62284	3·50265	3·38964	3·28324
17	4·57551	4·39077	4·21904	4·05911	3·90993	3·77052	3·64003	3·51769	3·40282	3·29480
18	4·60786	4·41866	4·24312	4·07993	2·92794	3·78815	3·65357	3·52945	3·41304	3·30369
19	4·63460	4·44152	4·26270	4·09672	3·94235	3·79851	3·66422	3·53863	3·42026	3·31053
20	4·65669	4·46027	4·27862	4·11026	3·95388	3·80834	3·67262	3·54580	3·42710	3·31579

Index

(*ref.* denotes references in text)

More about Penguins and Pelicans

Some books on Business and Management published by Penguins

Systems Thinking   *F. E. Emery*
The Business of Management   *Roger Falk*
Behavioral Science in Management   *Saul Gellerman*
The Modern Business Enterprise   *Michael Gilbert (Ed)*
Integrated Marketing   *B. G. S. James*
Management and Machiavelli   *Anthony Jay*
Corporation Man   *Anthony Jay*
Industrialism and Industrial Man   *Clark Kerr,*
    John T. Dunlop, Frederick Harbison and C. A. Myers
Management and the Social Sciences   *Tom Lupton*
Payment Systems   *Tom Lupton (Ed)*
Trade Unions   *W. E. J. McCarthy (Ed)*
Management Decisions and the Role of Forecasting
    James Morrell
Systems Analysis   *Stanford L. Optner*
Understanding Company Financial Statements
    R. H. Parker
Writers on Organizations   *D. S. Pugh, D. J. Hickson and*
    C. R. Hinings
Organization Theory   *D. S. Pugh*

Some books on Business and Management published by Penguins